PERSEVERANCE

Growing up Cherokee

A novel by John Martin

TABLE OF CONTENTS

This book is dedicated to all who are going through difficult times. Persevere! Things will get better. It is also dedicated to my phenomenal high school track coach, Bob LeSueur, whose life lessons have influenced me every day of my life. And, to my parents, who overcame so many hardships. You were the definition of perseverance.

Special thanks to Velva, Megan and Jai Powell, and to Casey Galbraith for their assistance in making this book a reality.

Print ISBN: 978-1-54397-518-5

eBook ISBN: 978-1-54397-519-2

CHAPTER 1

BELONGING

S tanding alone in the dark, at first, I saw only dust particles danc-
ing in sunlight beams between the old, ragged blinds and the edges
of the windows. After my eyes adjusted, I saw all the beds. Metal-
framed bunk beds were lined up along the walls. They were old, rusted
brown, many with broken springs hanging down. Old, thin worn-out grey
cotton mattresses with blue stripes and the little "buttons" that poked into
one's ribs were rolled up on most of the beds. The air was stale, smelling
of mildew, and the only sound was dripping water far off around a dimly
lit corner. "What am I doing here?" I whispered aloud. I carefully walked
toward the light and the smell of mildew became strong and the sound of
slowly dripping water became louder. As I rounded the corner, I entered an
old, dilapidated bathroom. The sink was filled with the pipes that should
have been connected to the wall. Following the sound of the dripping,
I pulled back an old, mildew covered shower curtain to see a mildewed
showerhead dripping water onto a green stained drain. The shower floor
and walls were made of small tiles, many broken and discolored. "I don't
belong here," I thought.

I turned around and found my way back to the doorway of the main room, leaving the mildew, dust and darkness behind. A large hallway extended to the left, but I heard sounds come from down the hallway in front of me. As I walked forward, the old, grey, cracked tile floor gave way to a polished marble floor. The lighting became bright and the air smelled clean. Hope rose within me, but I still did not understand where I was or why I was there. Further down the hall were two nice, polished elevators with live plants on either side of them.

Breathing several sighs of relief, I heard sounds from a room around the corner. Carrying my small suitcase, I entered the brightly lit room. The air was fresh and everything was clean; spotless. "This is where I belong," I thought as I breathed a deep sigh of relief. On each new, wood-framed bunk bed was a nice new thick, plush mattress and clean sheets and a boy my age. Two white women in nice uniforms were cleaning. Nobody noticed me in the room. I noticed it seemed strange that all the other boys were white with light skin and blonde hair, blue eyes and clean clothes. They all were reading brand new books. As I rounded the set of bunks in the middle of the room, I saw one bed was empty. It was a top bunk in the center of the beautiful room. The boy on the bottom bunk looked up at me for a moment then, without a word, looked away and continued reading.

I happily placed my small suitcase on the top bunk, climbed the nice, new polished wooden ladder and sat on the bed. "This is so nice," I thought. I couldn't help smiling as I ran my hand across the rung of the newly polished ladder.

Suddenly, one of the cleaning ladies rushed over to the bed I had sat on and glared at me with her teeth clenched and fury in her eyes. "Who are you and how did you get in here?" she demanded.

"I was in the wrong room. I found this room and…"

"Quiet!" she sternly ordered. "Clara, get him off of there and back where he belongs at once. Now we'll have to strip this bed down and wash everything. Just get this one out of here."

"But nobody was using it. Why can't I stay? I was…"

"Down! Get down now!" shouted the woman.

Shaking and confused, I climbed down. My voice trembling, asked, "Where do I go?"

"Back to the room you belong."

"That room is dirty and empty. Nobody's there."

"That is your problem. You don't belong here."

The other woman approached me, and a gnarled hand at the end of a bony arm reached for my shaking arm, and she grabbed it.

Suddenly I awoke, sitting up in bed. I was breathing hard, my pulse racing and sweat pouring down my face, soaking my straight black hair and brown skin. Wiping my face with the sheet, I felt frustration and anger that I kept having this same dream. "Why? What does this mean?" I thought. I lay back down and tried to go back to sleep. I could not sleep, but thought about the recurring bad dream until it was time to get up for school.

CHAPTER 2

A ROUGH BEGINNING

My name is John and this is my story. It was October of 1960, the time of year when the southern Appalachian region explodes into an array of fall colors. Green turns myriad shades of reds, yellows, and oranges. The mornings are fresh and crisp and the afternoons warm and comfortable with gentle winds and turquoise blue skies almost every day.

My dad, Jim had just become a father. "You have a strong baby boy and your wife is just fine," the doctor told him. Jim's face lit up and he smiled a huge smile. The doctor continued, "Jim, I don't think that boy got a drop of white blood. He's all Indian."

Jim quickly walked to the nursery to look through the window. There I was…Jim's boy. Long black hair hung all the way down to my lower back. Jim's dark brown eyes filled with tears of joy.

Dad was fairly tall, almost six feet and he weighed about one-hundred-eighty pounds. He had brown skin, dark eyes and straight black hair.

He was athletic and enjoyed many sports, though his favorite sport by far was baseball. Even though he did not grow up in Knoxville, Tennessee, he was well known in the local baseball community. He had played baseball on scholarship at the University of Tennessee, where he played successfully for all four years of his college career. He lived in a dorm room in the football stadium on the University of Tennessee campus and had many friends on the baseball and football teams. Even though he was one of only a few Native Americans on campus, he had truly loved his college days.

After college Dad was drafted into the US Army where he served as a sergeant in the 101st Airborne Division, the Screaming Eagles. He was a combat veteran of the Korean War, but would not speak of the things he had seen or done while on the Korean Peninsula. On rare occasion he would awaken during the night with flashbacks from the war and he would, at times, burst into fits of rage for little or no apparent reason, but he was never violent physically.

He was known to be somewhat stubborn when he thought he or someone he cared about was being treated unfairly. He had a temper within, but controlled it quite well. His Indian friends would call him "the Angry War Chief" when he was fuming, and that was their way of telling him to calm down. Dad's non-Indian friends just told him to calm down. But, most of the time Dad was calm and collected.

Dad was Cherokee, one-half to be exact, and my mother, Becky was of Irish descent. Dad could prove his blood quantum through old tribal rolls, which were official lists of tribal members.

Dad's parents and grandparents had all passed away before I was born so, sadly, I would only know them through stories and pictures. Mom's parents were both still living in a small community in the Southern Appalachians. In Tennessee everybody said "y'all," but in North Carolina everybody said "y'uns." For years, I could not be sure where my grandparents lived because Grandpa always said "y'uns" but Grammy would say "y'all." It didn't matter to me, though, as long as I was in the southern Appalachian Mountains.

Dad's only living relatives lived in western North Carolina on the Qualla Boundary, what most people called the Cherokee Indian Reservation. The sovereign nation of 100 square miles was once a part of 140,000 square miles throughout eight present-day southern states where the flourishing native people dominated the southern Appalachians dating back thousands of years. The Boundary had always been a significant part of Dad's life, and he would make sure it was a part of mine as well. To him, the Boundary was sacred land where the bones of his ancestors were buried and permeated the very plants and animals themselves, reminding him of all who had gone before.

Dad co-owned a hardware store in Knoxville, Tennessee, along with his friend Brady Frederick, whom Dad considered to be a very good friend. Dad had worked for a tool company, but when he consistently out-sold representatives in all the other regions, rather than rewarding him, the company cut Dad's territory in half. So, Dad quit, took what money he had saved, teamed up with Brady and they opened a small hardware store of their own. The store was not associated with any national chain, but it did good business. Dad was good with tools and he and Brady were known for their good advice and honesty. The store, called Frederick Hardware, was in a brick building next to Kingston Pike, the main highway running through the western part of the county. In the front of the store were small items such as bags of grass seed, garden hoses, gloves and bird seed. The aisles to the left held small gardening tools and a variety of vegetable seeds. Electrical and plumbing supplies were about halfway to the back of the store. On the right side were power tools such as drills and saws, hammers, screwdrivers, levels and the nails, screws and other small things that were used with them. Near the back were bulk items; plywood, two by fours and other pieces of building material, chain-link fencing and cement. In the very back was the paint section with gallons of paint in many colors and all the items needed to complete a painting job. To the side of the paint were the ladders. Dad liked to prop one of the front doors open to allow fresh air to circulate throughout the store.

Mom preferred to stay at home. She was an excellent gardener and grew green beans, squash and other vegetables during the summer, then canned them in mason jars so the family would have homegrown all year long. She was a strong woman, both physically and emotionally. She loved Dad and me with all her heart and worked diligently to provide a wonderful home for us.

We were a happy family and lived in a neighborhood, Kingston Pike Estates, in the west side of Knox County. Our house was on Diana Lane. As far as we knew, we were the only American Indian family in the area, something that bothered Dad. He was determined I would know my Cherokee culture and history, so we spent a lot time with our relatives on the Boundary. Qualla Boundary was the actual name, but most locals called it the Boundary. Non-Indians usually knew the Boundary as the Cherokee Indian Reservation.

I had a difficult start in life. When I was only a few days old I had to have surgery to repair a hernia. And, for the first couple of years of my life, I had breathing problems. Shortly before my third birthday, I woke during the night and could barely breathe due to congested lungs. I heard my parents talking downstairs, so I slowly climbed out of bed and managed to walk down the stairs, becoming dizzy with every step. When my mother saw me, she gasped.

"Jim! He's turning blue!"

Mom grabbed me up into her arms while Dad phoned the pediatrician, Dr. Caiden Landis. Dr. Landis was a tall, strong man with wavy brown hair and a wide smile who had a calming, reassuring personality, and anyone who had ever met the Landis family absolutely loved them. Dad's mother had refused to ever see a doctor or take Dad to a doctor when he was a boy, because she did not trust modern medicine. So, for Dad to trust a doctor, the doctor had to be remarkable, and Dr. Landis certainly was.

It was a very cold night outside, which proved to be very fortunate for me. Dr. Landis told Dad to run steaming hot water in the shower to create a steam room. He said to keep me in the steam for five minutes, then take me out into the cold air for five minutes and repeat the process until I coughed up the congestion in my lungs. Dad did as Dr. Landis directed.

Mom, with tears running down her face, managed to hold her emotions in check as she followed Dad every step of the way. At first nothing improved and I was limp in Dad's arms. But Dad trusted Dr. Landis and kept it up for almost thirty minutes. I suddenly coughed up all sorts of mucus from my lungs and the next morning felt fine. Dad, on the other hand, developed a terrible cold and ended up missing three days of work.

When I was five years old, I began having stomach aches and other pains. After examinations by several doctors, my parents were told I had problems with my digestive tract and that my little body was having difficulty digesting certain proteins. They were not sure exactly what was causing it, and I ended up in the hospital for two weeks and had to return every month for a year afterward. I was put on a special diet of fresh fruits and vegetables cooked with no oils, and nothing fried was allowed. Mom and Dad were also told to serve no processed foods, and no carbonated or sugary drinks were to be served to me. Water was to be the only liquid. The only meat I could eat was to be virtually fat free. The diet worked and my pains were finally, after more than a year, a thing of the past.

After experiencing these and other physical hardships at a young age, I had developed a sense of resilience. I knew at an early age that life could be hard, but I also learned I could overcome adversity. I was a born survivor.

CHAPTER 3

RABID CHANGE

When I was five years old, life was calm at home. The only things to the west of our house were forests and farms. Almost all of the farms grew corn. Yellow corn, white corn and sometimes beans and melons were grown on the farms. A few farms raised chickens, cows and pigs. Mom liked having the farms nearby because she could always get as much produce as needed for canning to last throughout the winter. I preferred the forests and often climbed trees or spent hours looking for interesting rocks to take home.

Wild honeysuckle grew profusely about a half mile down the road from our house along an old, long forgotten fence line that was part of an abandoned farm. I enjoyed getting on my bicycle, which had a dark blue frame, a white banana-shaped seat and large U-shaped handlebars. I loved to ride to the end of the street, turn right and then simply glide down Kingsridge Drive, the long, gently sloping road while listening to the whirring sound of the tires and feeling the wind on my face. The first time I noticed the old farm I saw the old, abandoned house. I walked through the tall grass, up the wooden steps onto the front porch and entered, as the front door was gone. The house was empty. The old, dusty wooden floor made a creaking sound with every step and I noticed it had no electrical outlets, no places for lights on the ceilings, not even a sink or bathtub. I liked the house and rode home to tell my Dad all about it. Dad, however, was not amused and ordered me to not go in the old house ever again.

"But Dad," I argued, "It's really neat inside."

"It may be neat, but old houses can be dangerous. You could fall through the floor and get hurt and nobody would be there to help you. You're not to go in it again," he sternly stated.

"But Dad!"

"No buts, John. Do you understand me?"

"Fine. But can I still go to the honeysuckle?"

To this, Dad agreed.

I often visited the honeysuckle bushes and would pull the stems out of the buds and taste the sweet nectar. I noticed some of the honeysuckle flowers were white, others a yellow color. The nectar from the white flowers was always sweeter, so I preferred to taste them. I did not mind sharing the honeysuckle with the bees, and the bees never seemed to be bothered by me, as they never stung. I liked watching the bees buzz from flower to flower collecting pollen or eating nectar. Bees fascinated me, and I never understood why the white kids always ran off screaming as soon as they saw bees. After several visits to the honeysuckle, I was the only kid in the neighborhood who would go near the bushes. I did not mind that because it meant things would be quieter and I could listen to the buzzing of the bees, the wind in the trees, the songs of birds and other sounds of nature I so enjoyed.

We lived in a split-level house. The front of the house was brick and the rest of the sides were wood, which Dad had painted light brown. The driveway sloped down from the road into a carport, and a sidewalk connected the driveway to a small rectangular concrete porch in front of the front door. The side door, which connected the carport to the downstairs living room, was used more than the front door. The downstairs living room had a small bathroom with only a sink and a toilet, and the laundry room was next to the bathroom. A back door led outside from the laundry room. A small set of stairs led up to the kitchen and a small dining room. The dining room door opened to a concrete patio with concrete stairs that descended to the yard and black iron rails surrounded both the small patio and stairs. Outside the kitchen was the living room that led to the top floor where my bedroom was on the right with a window facing out the front of the house. A second bedroom was used for guests and the master bedroom was across the hall from my room. The master bedroom had a small bathroom with a sink and a toilet which connected to the room with the bathtub. That room connected to yet another, slightly larger bathroom with a sink, a toilet, and a large closet. Mom used the larger bathroom and Dad used the small one. I would use any bathroom that was unoccupied when I needed to go.

The house had a black and white Zenith television with three channels available; NBC, ABC and CBS. My favorite television show was Batman. I would sit on the floor with my legs folded under my body and carefully watch all the action. Because Batman showed the first half of a show one night and the conclusion the following night, I often worried the criminals would win. Dad always assured me that Batman would always beat the criminals.

In the summer of 1965, reports began to surface of rabid foxes in the area. It turned out rabid bats had bitten foxes, and the foxes had begun attacking other wild animals, farm animals and even people's pets. An article in the local newspaper even showed a fox had attacked a man's truck as he drove down Kingston Pike, the main highway that connected downtown Knoxville to the west end of the county. In fact, our house was about two-hundred yards from Kingston Pike and I could often hear cars and trucks driving by. After the report of the rabid fox attacking the truck, Dad put up a chain-link fence all the way around the back yard. He told me to stay close to the house and if I ever saw a fox or any animal acting strangely to get inside immediately and tell someone. I liked the fence. It made me feel safe from rabid animals, plus it was fun to climb.

Mom caught me climbing the fence one day.

"John!" she shouted across the yard. "Don't climb on the fence. You'll get hurt."

"I won't get hurt. I'm a good climber!" I replied.

"No more climbing. Use the gates."

I agreed, but often climbed the fence when I knew my mother was not watching. I also never got hurt.

I wanted a puppy. Dad liked basset hounds and we soon found just the right one. On the way home with the new puppy I observed its ears were very droopy.

"That's it!" Dad exclaimed. "We'll call her Droopy."

I learned to love Droopy and Droopy loved me. We spent many afternoons and weekends running and playing in the fenced in back yard. When allowed in the house, Droopy would often roll over onto her back. I thought it was funny and would pet her stomach.

In April of that year a shopping center was built only a few miles east of our house. It was called Suburban Center. Mom said it would save a lot of time because it was far closer to the house than any other shopping center. It had an A&P grocery store, Cooper's Barber Shop, a drug store and a small toy store called L&L Toys. A Gulf gas station was built across the street from the shopping center.

I loved going to the shopping center with Dad on Saturday mornings. On a typical Saturday we would stop by the drug store and drink a cherry Coke at the store's fountain. I liked the stools at the fountain. They had silver bases and soft, red plastic cushions to sit on. My favorite thing to do on the stools was to spin in circles. Spinning was fun and I never got dizzy.

The lady behind the counter was nice and always put a little extra squirt of cherry syrup in my Coke. She was a middle-aged woman with light brown hair and she always wore a white apron and a small white paper hat. As she began to prepare my cherry Coke, she would look around as if sneaking, look at me, wink as if she was doing a huge favor and then add the extra cherry syrup. I thought it was funny and smiled. When she handed the cherry coke to me, she would whisper, "Our secret." I took the comment seriously and shook my head in agreement; something that always brought a chuckle from Dad. After our time together at the drug store, Dad and I would shop for groceries. I enjoyed pushing the shopping cart, but always had trouble stopping it and repeatedly hit him in the back of the legs when he stopped to look at something. After the grocery store, Dad would stop at the gas station to gas up the car. I liked it when the car ran across the black hose that made a bell ring. Men would come out, raise the car's hood, check the oil, wash the windows and pump the gas. The men all wore grey pants and blue shirts. Each man's name was sewn just above the front pocket, and every one of them had an old rag hanging out of a back pocket of their pants. I noticed they all had dirty hands and grease under their fingernails. They seemed to have a dirty job, but they were always smiling and laughing. The men and Dad would enjoy a talk, but my favorite thing to do at the gas station was to get out of the car and jump up and down on the black hose, trying to make it ring the bell. For some reason, I could never get it to ring.

Although I looked forward to Saturday mornings spent with my dad, I did not look forward to the Saturdays that I knew were haircut days. The barbers at Cooper's Barber Shop were nice, but I simply did not like getting my hair cut. My straight black hair always would look the same, as far as I was concerned; straight and black and messed up every time the wind blew. So, I saw no point in cutting my hair. Unfortunately, Mom disagreed and would tell us when it was time for me to get another haircut. The rare Saturdays when I got to go to the toy store, however, I would wake up eager to go. The store was small. It had a heavy glass front door which I found very difficult to push open. As soon as I entered, I noticed the aisles ran from the front of the store to the back. The toys I liked were on the lower shelves where I could reach them. I appreciated the man who owned the store making it easy to reach the good stuff. Toys for older kids were on higher shelves and out of the way. The old, brown metal cash register was on a glass counter next to the front door and the owner usually sat quietly on a stool behind the register. The first time Dad surprised me with a trip to the toy store, I bought a Mr. Potato Head, which I played with for great lengths of time. I would tire of putting the eyes, lips, ears feet and hair in the same correct places every time, so I liked to mix Mr. Potato Head up. My favorite was to put the eyes where the ears belonged, the ears where the eyes belonged, and making the lips and hair trade places. To me, it was funny and I would always run to my Dad to show off the mixed-up Mr. Potato Head.

One Saturday evening Dad had to go to the grocery store for something that Mom needed for dinner. Dad backed the car into a parking space next to the sidewalk in front of the A&P, pulled a handle below and left of the steering wheel that made clicking sounds as it came out, turned to me and stated, "John, stay in the car and no matter what you do, do not pull this handle."

Dad left the car. The only thing I could think about was not pulling the handle. I sat and stared at it, wondering why my dad had said that. After what seemed to be a long, long time, I slid across the front seat and took hold of the handle. I did not mean to do anything, but as soon as I twisted it just a bit, it popped back into its original position and the car slowly began to roll. I stood up on the seat, put both hands on the steering wheel and watched helplessly as the car continued to roll across the parking lot.

"Daddy?" I called.

"Daddy, where are you?"

"Daddy, make the car stop." But Daddy was inside the grocery store.

"Daddy … " Bump! The car had stopped. It had rolled into the concrete base of one of the shopping center's parking lot light poles. I stood still, staring forward. The car door opened and there stood Dad, and he was not smiling. I sat down, slumped over and slowly slid back across the seat to where I was supposed to be.

Dad got in, teeth clenched, looking straight ahead. His face was red. He took a deep breath, sighed, looked sternly at me and shook his finger at me. I knew I was in big trouble. But, as was his nature, instead of yelling at me, he mumbled something about "shouldn't have said that" and then drove home. I said nothing on the drive home, only wondering what would happen to me. When we arrived home, Dad calmly told Mom that I had had my first driving lesson. I did not understand what that meant, but was glad I was not in trouble and went upstairs to play with Mr. Potato Head.

CHAPTER 4

ANDREW

I was in second grade when one evening my parents told me to sit down because they had something exciting to tell me. I sat on the plush French provincial couch in the living room.

"We loved each other enough to bring you into this world. Do you understand?" Dad asked.

"No. What does you two loving each other have to do with me being born?" I asked in a puzzled voice. In my young mind if a couple agreed to have a baby, then the Mommy would have a baby; very simple.

Mom and Dad looked at one another, not sure how to respond. I stared at them in complete confusion. After a few awkward moments, Mom stated, "You are going to have a little brother!"

"When?!" I exclaimed as I sprang from the couch and jumped up and down with excitement.

"In about four months." Mom replied through a wide smile.

"But why so long, Mommy?"

"The baby has to grow inside of me until he's big enough to be born, sweetheart." she lovingly said.

Dad added, "We're naming him Andrew after my stepfather."

The weeks seemed to pass slowly, but I was phenomenally excited, telling everyone at school and even strangers my parents and I would meet in public. Mom and Dad were preparing the nursery in what had been the guest room and I always wanted to help, so they would often give me small jobs to do. My favorite task was to bring in Droopy every day to show her the progress. The closer the due date, sometime in late May, the more excited I became.

March 23 arrived and to my surprise Dad came to school to check me out early. We walked to the car. I asked why I was being checked out early, but Dad remained silent until we were in the car and driving home.

"John," Dad solemnly stated, "your mother lost the baby."

Completely confused, I protested, "But how can she lose the baby? He's inside her."

After a short pause, Dad forced himself to say, "The baby died this morning."

"What?! How? What happened?" I asked as my eyes began to fill with tears.

"Our blood types. I am O-positive and your mother is O-negative. The doctors said the Rh factors caused something to go terribly wrong," Dad tried to explain.

I could not understand what dad was talking about and just stared forward through the tears.

"You are never to speak of it. It would upset your mother. Do you understand me?"

I sat in stunned silence, not knowing what to think but feeling my world had just fallen apart. My plans to teach Andrew to play ball, play with Droopy, run, ride bikes and all things boys do were shattered forever.

Dad continued, "Your mother will be in the hospital about a week. I will take down the nursery before she gets home."

"You mean I'm not going to have a brother?" I asked.

"No. Never. We can never have another baby. Doctor's orders."

I was more upset than at any time in my young life and desperately wanted to talk about it so I could understand it all, but dared not since Dad had ordered me to never speak of it.

For the next week Dad took me to a local fast food restaurant for breakfast before driving me to school. I knew not to mention Andrew to anyone, but each morning I told the teacher how my daddy had taken me out to eat breakfast. Near the end of the week I looked up to see Dad and my teacher talking in the hallway. I could not hear what was being said, but saw my teacher, Mrs. Russell's mouth suddenly drop open as she quickly raised her hand to cover it. Dad took me home, but not one word was spoken the entire way.

After I walked into the house, I discovered Mom sitting up in bed. She slowly arose, walked to me, hugged me and whispered, "I love you, John."

"I love you too, Mommy." I replied, but dared not ask any questions or mention Andrew. I put my things away, went outside and pet Droopy to find what little solace I could. I felt devastated and knew nothing would ever be able to replace my little brother, Andrew.

CHAPTER 5

LANGUAGE ARTS AND SUNDAY SCHOOL

I t was the fall of 1968 and third grade had started. The school, Maple Ridge, had grades one through eight and was a fairly new school building. The school was built on a large field next to a narrow two-lane road with no markings. Forests and caves were to the south of the school property. A new neighborhood was being built to the east and a horse farm was just across the road to the east. A few farms were located to the west.

The school building had marble-looking floors and the walls had thick, heavy, yellow tiles from the floor up to about five feet high on the walls. The lights were bright. The hallways were wide and straight with classroom doors on each side. Every wing had bathrooms, which never smelled very good. The windows in the classrooms were made of horizontal pieces of thick glass. The teacher could turn a handle to open them to let in fresh air. Lockers were just inside each classroom against the hallway wall. The classroom floors were grey tiles with small streaks of black spattered across them. Each room had a long counter with a sink at the end and the chalk boards covered one entire wall. A wooden speaker was above the chalk board so the principal could make announcements. No two clocks in the building showed the same time, so all the students ignored them, except when the faster ones showed 3:30, as that was the time school was to end each day. They would then try to convince the teacher to allow them to immediately leave.

I was in Mrs. Klein's third-grade class. She did not like third graders. Mrs. Klein was sort of plump and had brown, hair that appeared to be shaped like a hornet's nest and a mean stare that could scare any third grader. Almost all the kids at Maple Ridge were white and rich. Scotty and I were the only Indian kids in the school. One kid, Roberto, was from Mexico. The white kids' families all drove new cars and the kids always had new clothes and shoes. Scotty and I rode the bus to school and none of the other students knew of the old cars our families owned. When my shoes got worn out the white kids would always ask why I didn't get new ones. Neither Scotty nor I would answer because then the other kids would know our families didn't have much money. Scotty and I hung around together a lot. Roberto would notice our clothes and shoes, but he never asked questions. He seemed to know why.

During language arts, the class had been studying root words. Mrs. Klein would say, "lovable", the root word is love and it means, able to be loved." "Beautiful" meant full of beauty. I was good at figuring out what words meant.

Unfortunately, Mrs. Klein often got Scotty mixed up with me. She would look directly at me and ask for an answer, saying, "Scotty, what's the answer?" We both just looked at her because we didn't know who she really wanted to give the answer. Many times, she would look at Scotty and say, "Answer the question, John." We were both afraid to answer because we didn't want her to be mad. I overheard Mrs. Klein telling Mrs. Simmons, another teacher in the school, that "Indians all look alike and should never be in the same class." Both Scotty and I hoped we would be moved to a nicer teacher's room, but we were never so lucky.

Mom, Dad and I attended a small Southern Baptist church down the road. Most of the families were white and some were extremely wealthy. They always seemed to stick together. Most of the rich people never paid much attention to our family. I asked Dad why that was and he just shook his head and said that money pays the bills. I didn't understand what he meant by that, but by the look on his Dad's face, I knew not to ask anything else for the moment.

A tall, white woman named Mrs. Gaul, who never smiled, ran the Sunday school. Everyone sat in straight rows of folding chairs and was told to be still and quiet and to listen to everything she said. Mrs. Gaul always wore the same light blue polyester dress to church, but never had on the same pair of shoes. Her hair was similar in shape to Mrs. Klein's, except Mrs. Gaul's hair was shaped more like a bee hive. It also changed colors from time to time. Sometimes it was light brown, sometimes dark brown, but my favorite was when it looked like rust. It reminded me of the copper wire and pipes I had seen at the hardware store. Whenever Mrs. Gaul said something really important, she would quickly shake her from head side to side, but her hair kept wiggling even after her head stopped. And strangely, it never changed shape. This amazed me, because my straight black hair was always untidy.

The junior department at church, where third and fourth graders attended, had been studying the Ten Commandments. Week after week, another commandment with long, boring explanations would be presented. Most of the children found it difficult to stay awake. Mrs. Gaul never did explain what thou or shalt meant, but she talked forever about what each commandment meant. She told the children if they broke the commandments that they would burn in hell forever. Then, she would assure everyone that God loved us, which was confusing to me.

One Sunday I figured out a commandment without Mrs. Gaul's explanation. That morning she started with the commandment, "Thou shalt not commit adultery!" She said it loud, slow and harsh. Then she went right on to the next commandment. No long, boring explanation about adultery, no examples, not even the threat of going to hell. This is when I remembered Mrs. Klein's lessons on figuring words out.

"*Adultery; the root word has to be adult.*" I thought. "*An adult is a grown-up.*" I thought. "*So, that commandment must mean it's a sin to become a grown-up? But that's impossible. How can anybody not turn into a grown-up? No wonder she skipped over it so fast. That must not be an important commandment.*" I was very proud I had figured it out.

I was so excited about figuring out the commandment I never did hear another word Mrs. Gaul said the rest of Sunday school. When Sunday school ended, I really wanted to impress Mrs. Gaul with how smart I was.

"*Maybe she'll finally smile.*" I thought as I scampered up to her. "Mrs. Gaul!" She did not respond. She did that a lot when I spoke to her. So, I said it louder, but still no reply. Finally, I tugged on her blue polyester dress and said excitedly, "Mrs. Gaul!"

"What is it, John?"

"My parents committed adultery."

"What? Well, I don't want to know about it!" she gruffly said as she stared down at me with her cold, unfeeling blue eyes.

"Well they did, and so did you!"

"I never!" she exclaimed.

"Yes, you did. Everybody does. You can't help it," I explained.

"Oh, you little heathen! You people may…oh never mind!" and she stomped away in disgust.

I left Sunday school very confused that she would get so mad because I had been smart enough to figure out a commandment.

In the car on the way home Mom asked Dad, "Do you know why Martha Gaul was so cold to us today?"

"I have no idea. It was strange, though." Dad replied.

I remained silent.

CHAPTER 6

THE WELL AND THE SMOKEHOUSE

om's parents lived up in the southern Appalachian Mountains in a very small community called Lucas Creek. The main road through the community was paved, but all the other roads were gravel or dirt. The houses were almost all very small and made of wood, some with what appeared to be black paper on the outside. Grandpa called it tar paper. The houses near the main road had electricity, but I had been told the houses further away had none. The only business in the community was a very small grocery store with a screen door and a very cranky old man behind the counter named Mr. Packer. Every time I was sent to pick up something from the store, Mr. Packer would yell, "Hurry up and shut the door, boy!" I would get what I had been sent to buy and leave as quickly as possible. The store was even smaller than the toy store back home, it was dimly lit, and the only electrical item besides the lights was a small freezer, which Mr. Packer refused to let children open. The floor was wood and it squeaked with every step. It was also very dusty.

Grandpa was Scots-Irish and Grammy was Irish. I liked to visit for a day or two, but after that it became boring. I had no one to play with and I missed Droopy. If cousin Pricilla was there, I wanted to leave immediately.

Grandpa told the story of how he had gone west years earlier and earned degrees in math and chemistry from the University of Oklahoma. He was very proud of his accomplishment. I wanted to one day attend the University of Tennessee, where both my parents had graduated. Dad had told many wonderful stories of college and I wanted to be like him and go to UT.

Grandpa taught school a few miles from the house in the mountains. The school was a small, white, one-room school with large windows on the sides. It also served as Lucas Creek's church and had a small steeple on the roof. Grandpa taught all the students, who were in multiple grades. Grandpa was a short, strong man with grey hair who always spoke calmly. He drove an old black and white 1958 Chevrolet car and he drove very slowly.

Behind the house, Grandpa had built a smokehouse and had used it for years.

"You can always tell a smokehouse from the outside," Grandpa stated.

"How?"

"Look at it carefully. What's unusual about it?"

"Well, it's small."

"Don't just see it, John. Look at it carefully."

The smokehouse was built of thick logs, cracked by years of weathering, but still solid and strong. The roof was covered with split cedar shingles, many covered with moss. No nails had been used to hold the logs together. Grandpa told me he had used notching, which made the logs fit together like a puzzle. Grandpa said he had used half-dovetail notching. Between the weathered logs was what grandpa called chinking, a mix of red clay and straw. The chinking was mostly still there except for a few places where it had broken off and been patched with cement. Even though the smokehouse was very old it still stood strong.

My eyes widened. "It's white on the bottom part and black on top!"

"Exactly."

"But why?"

"I used salt to cure the meats and then smoked them after I hung 'em up. Over the years the salt and smoke colored the building." Grandpa explained that a salt solution was rubbed into fresh meat to preserve it, as no one had refrigerators back in what I called "the old days." Grandpa said the smoke from the hardwood fire kept bugs away from the meat and added flavor to the meat as well.

Grandpa and I walked to the smokehouse. A slight breeze blew, the weeds crunched under our feet and the sound of wasps that had a nest under one corner of the roof could be heard. Grandpa opened the door. Inside was dark and dusty. Cobwebs swung back and forth as the breeze entered the smokehouse and dust and dirt rose from the floor for a momentary dance. Slight beams of sunlight shone through small holes in the chinking and the air was cool with the smell of dust, old wood and moisture. After my eyes adjusted, I noticed the smokehouse was stacked almost full of wooden boxes.

"Where's the meat, Grandpa?" I asked.

Quietly laughing, Grandpa explained he had stopped smoking his own meat a few years back after the grocery store opened up in town.

"What's in the boxes?" I asked.

"Books. I love to read. Hope you do too, John. After I finish a stack of books, I box them up and store them in here. So far the salt has kept the bugs out." Grandpa liked reading books about people or places. Even though grandpa was Scots-Irish, he disliked most books written about American history because, as he had explained to me, they were not factual and always portrayed Indians as savage, stupid, or some kind of weird nobleman of the forests. Grandpa warned me not to believe everything I would be taught in school history classes.

We left the smokehouse and approached the house. Grammy was just coming outside to pick vegetables from the garden. Between the house and the smokehouse was a huge flat grey stone on the ground. "Grammy, what's the rock here for?" I asked.

"It covers an old well." She seemed to drift off into thought. "Some people told us to fill in the well after we got indoor plumbing, but you can't trust the Germans."

"What?" I asked, very puzzled by Grammy's remark.

"People have to have fresh water, John. If the Germans ever bombed us and blew up the water plant, we'd still have good water."

"But why would Germans bomb here? This is in the middle of nowhere. Besides, that war ended a million years ago."

"Still don't trust the Germans," Grammy said. Then Grammy and Mom went to the garden to pick corn, green beans and tomatoes for supper. Grammy was a wonderful cook. Her meals were always freshly cooked, usually with vegetables she had picked from the garden or canned earlier. Grammy made the best cakes I had ever eaten. The icing was especially delicious. Dad told me Grammy used lard in a lot of her cooking and that was why things were so tasty. But he had cautioned, lard was bad for the heart, so he told me not to get too used to eating it. Grammy always used the same dishes. They were white with blue drawings on them. The bowls matched and the forks, spoons and knives were always grey. The children drank from glass cups and the adults used small coffee cups that matched the plates and bowls.

Grandpa and I went back into the house. Grandpa sat in his old, wooden rocking chair and I sat on a footstool next to him. Grandpa picked up a newspaper and started to read. I looked around. Everything was just as I had remembered. A small wooden table stood next to the rocking chair. Grandpa had made the table himself. The legs were made of wooden spools thread came on. He had glued dozens together to make the legs. The top looked as if it had been the top of a wooden box. It was nailed to the legs. Grandpa always said to never throw anything away, because you never knew when you might need it. A small wooden radio was on the table and a black metal telephone sat next to the radio. A single light bulb hung down from the ceiling, giving off just enough light to see by at night. The house had no television and the radio picked up only one station.

I especially enjoyed the telephone. Sometimes I would slowly pick it up. Every time I did, I could hear two women talking. They always were telling things on other people in the community. Mom caught me listening in one day and scolded me.

"Hang that up!" she whispered in a stern voice.

I hung up. "Mom, every time I pick it up, two women are talking on the phone. I think there's something wrong with it."

"Nothing's wrong with it. It's a party line."

"What's a party line?"

"That's where a lot of houses have phones on the same line. If you pick it up and people are talking, you hang up and try again later."

"Well every time I pick it up it's the same two women talking about people."

"Then quit picking it up."

"Okay," I said.

Just then, my worst nightmare came true…Pricilla. She came barreling through the room on her way to the kitchen, almost knocking me down and yelling, "Where's the cake? I want some cake!"

I could not stand Pricilla. She was loud, crude, spoiled, selfish, and demanding and she thought she knew everything just because she was four years older than me. She also hated anything Indian. Pricilla was chubby with very pale skin, light brown hair and a few freckles on her face. She rarely smiled except when she was with her father, who Mom's sister had married. Pricilla's father's name was Phil. Phil was a tall, fat man who owned a small construction and remodeling company in the town they lived in. Phil had a lot of money, always drove new cars and lavished gifts upon Pricilla every chance he had. Phil often bragged about ways he made what he called "good money." He bragged one day over dinner how he would go to someone's house, tell them he needed to repair part of a door, take it back to his shop, spend two minutes working on it, then sit in his office for an hour or two smoking cigars and listening to the radio. He would then return to the customer's house and tell them what a difficult job it was and charge them extra. One of Phil's favorite tricks was keeping empty paint cans from many different colors of paint in the shop. He would send a crew out to paint a house, but hide empty paint cans of the color to be used that day in a truck. When the customer was not looking, the crew was instructed to lay the old empty cans out among the cans that had actually been used. Then they were to charge the customer for the paint and labor for all the cans. If a customer ever became suspicious, the crew would call Phil. Phil would rush to the scene, act deeply insulted, explain why so much paint had been needed, and if necessary, he would remind the customer he was a deacon down at the local church. Phil laughed and claimed he would have customers not only satisfied with the job, but even pay tips for having insulted the crew.

Dad disliked Phil as much as I disliked Pricilla. "Never treat people that way," Dad would always instruct me after Phil had told one of his stories.

Grammy and Mom were washing vegetables at the sink.

"Grammy, where's the cake?" Pricilla barked.

"Hello Pricilla," Grammy said as she walked over and hugged the little monster.

"I didn't have time to make one today, but …"

"Fine," Pricilla pouted. As she stomped away, Pricilla turned back toward the kitchen and demanded, "you didn't make me a cake, so the least you can do is make chuck wagon for dinner!"

"Pricilla," Grandpa said softly, "Show respect to your grandmother."

"You would have to show up," I said.

Pricilla looked down her nose at me and said, "Nothing you say can touch my virgin ears."

I briefly thought back to the time in Sunday school when the teacher was telling the story of the Virgin Mary. "Why do they call her Virgin Mary?" I had asked. The teacher had replied, "It's because she was a good, nice, sweet girl who did things that pleased God."

"*That sure doesn't sound like Pricilla*," I thought.

"Oh, virgin my foot!" I shouted as I laughed and reentered the kitchen.

Pricilla's mouth dropped open. Grammy heard what we had said and began to have one of her spells. Spells was what everybody called it when Grammy would suddenly become weak, place the back of her hand over her forehead and slump back into the nearest seat. I knew she was faking it just to get everybody's attention, but Dad had told me not to say anything, because it would upset Grammy and Mom. Grandpa just ignored the spells.

"Daddy, did you hear what John said?" Pricilla bellowed.

"John, just go outside. I'll take care of it," Dad said.

I shook my head, walked out the back door and sat on the porch, resting my chin in my hands while I waited for the commotion inside to stop.

I could hear everything that was happening inside…Grammy moaning, people running around, water being turned on in the sink.

"Calm down everyone," Dad ordered. "I'm sure there's a good explanation for all of this."

"Here, Mother," Mom said. "Drink this water."

Dad opened the back door and stood in the doorway so everyone could hear. "John, do you know what a virgin is?"

"Yes. The Sunday School teacher told us."

Glass shattered and water splashed back in the kitchen. "Now, Mother, calm down! Let Jim finish. I'll clean it up," Mom growled.

"John, what did they tell you?" Dad asked.

"A virgin is someone who's sweet and nice and does good things. No way Pricilla's a…"

"Okay! Thank you," Dad quickly stated as he closed the kitchen door.

The commotion seemed to stop, but I still did not want to go back inside.

The dinner that evening was chuck wagon, corn, beans and slices of tomato. Hardly a word was spoken. Every now and then Dad and Grandpa started to laugh, but would stop when Mom gave Dad the look, when her eyes opened wide, her lips pursed as she stared at him. Dad knew when Mom gave him the look, he was to just let it go.

Once dinner was finished and the dishes washed, dried and put away, Mom, Dad and I departed for home. *"Thank goodness,"* I thought, glad I was getting away from Pricilla.

After arriving back home, Dad announced Droopy was old enough to have puppies and since Droopy was a pure breed, Dad had sought out the best dog to be Droopy's mate. Several days later, Droopy and I were playing in the back yard when a man showed up with a very strong looking basset hound on a leash and some papers in his hand. I watched from a distance as Dad and the man talked. After several minutes Dad handed the man some money and the man handed the leash and papers to Dad. Then the man left.

Dad brought the strong dog over to Droopy and me. The strong dog and Droopy excitedly began sniffing each other and Dad informed me the strong dog's name was Garfunkel and would be Droopy's new mate. Mom came out to see what was happening and Dad proudly stated, "This is our new dog, Garfunkel."

"You mean we get to keep him?" I asked excitedly.

"Yes we do," stated Dad.

"Jim, how can we afford to buy another dog?" inquired Mom.

"Garfunkel's owner sold him to me for ten dollars," explained Dad. Mom looked suspicious so Dad continued. "Garfunkel's owner is getting a divorce and the judge ordered him to sell Garfunkel and give half the money to his wife, so he sold Garfunkel to me for ten dollars," Dad laughed.

I jumped for joy as now I had two wonderful basset hounds to love.

Every day after school, I would go outside and spend a great deal of time playing with Droopy and Garfunkel. The dogs' antics made me laugh and I felt on top of the world.

CHAPTER 7

THE DISCOVERY

G randpa and Grammy would visit Knoxville from time to time, but I noticed they never came together.

"Why don't Grandpa and Grammy ever visit at the same time?" I asked.

A bit surprised, Mom replied, "Never mind, John. And don't you ever ask them."

I was confused, so I went outside to ask Dad, who was checking the oil in the car. "There are some things you don't need to know," stated Dad.

"So it's like a secret?" I asked excitedly.

"John, forget about it. Drop it."

The next afternoon, Mom, Dad and I drove to the hardware store to pick up some paint supplies to paint my room. I was excited and always enjoyed going to dad's hardware store. The store always had a certain out-doors smell I liked. My favorite part of the store was the section with hand tools. I was not allowed to touch saws, axes, or other tools with blades, but I was thrilled to get to play with hammers, screwdrivers and other less-dangerous tools. The paint was near the back of the store and that day I selected a light green paint. No matter how hard Mom tried to talk me out of it, I refused to change to another color. Dad laughed at the entire scene.

"Let the boy have a green room if he wants it," Dad laughed.

"How about a nice blue?" Mom urged.

"Green," I said.

"Well at least pick a different shade of green, John. That green is hard on the eyes."

"Not on my eyes, mom!"

"Okay. Fine. That green it is," Mom sighed.

I smiled and looked at Dad, who chuckled.

We also picked up a few brushes, pans and other items for the painting job. I insisted on carrying both gallons of paint to the car. I quickly realized the wire handles were very painful in my hands and the cans were heavy and hurting my shoulders. But that did not stop me. I waddled as fast as I could to the car and placed the cans on the ground next to the back of the car.

On the drive home, as I was rubbing my hands trying to get the red lines caused by the wire handles to disappear, I glanced out the window and spotted Grandpa's car parked at an apartment complex. I was very excited. "Hey, look! That's Grandpa's car! Let's go see him!" I exclaimed.

"Be quiet, John," Dad stated in a low, guarded voice.

"But…"

"Quiet!" Dad barked.

Mom began to cry.

"When will Grandpa be at the house?" I asked excitedly.

"He won't, John. Now drop it. Talk about something else," Dad ordered.

"But why would Grandpa come to town and not visit us?" I asked.

"Zip it now!" ordered Dad in a loud, stern voice.

I felt totally confused. Dad sped up and drove straight home.

I knew something had to be wrong but could not figure out what it could be. As the car stopped in the driveway, Mom bolted from her seat and ran sobbing into the house.

"Daddy?" I asked. "What's going on?"

Dad said nothing until we were inside the house. He reached over and turned on the television. "Just stay here and watch TV. And do not come upstairs," he directed.

Dad hurried upstairs. I could hear him close the bedroom door and lock it. The TV was playing, but I just sat, stunned. Time stood still and I was worried and confused.

After what seemed like hours, Dad came back downstairs. "John, sit down."

"I am sitting."

"Look. I'm going to tell you something that you can never repeat."

I looked at him out of the corner of my eyes with a look of suspicion on my face.

"Your mother's father, over the years, has had girlfriends. And some-times he visits them. It's very upsetting to your mother. So please, never speak of it. Understand?"

"I guess. Does Grammy know about it?"

"Yes, John. She knows."

"Well now it makes sense!"

"What makes sense?"

"Those two women on the telephone party line. They kept talking about Grandpa and Grammy arguing about what he did when he went on business trips."

"Oh John. Whatever you do, never repeat that. Please."

"Okay. But why would Grandpa want girlfriends when he's already married? Grownups can be weird."

"True. But, from now on, not one single word about any of this. You promise? Can I have your word on this, son?"

"Yes sir. I promise."

"Good. Thank you."

Dad went back upstairs. I could still hear Mom crying.

"I'll never forgive him. Never!" Mom yelled.

CHAPTER 8

THE COST OF AN UNFORGIVING HEART

After I learned of Grandpa and Grammy's problem, things were never the same. Grammy would visit and Mom invited her to stay for weeks at a time, much to Dad's desire for the opposite. But, when Grandpa would stop by, Mom would tell him, "You can stay one night. I want you out of this house tomorrow morning." She always said it in a very mean way. Soon, I was not allowed to spend much time with Grandpa at all.

Things continued in this manner for a couple of years. Then, one night, just as I was in my bedroom getting ready for bed the phone rang downstairs. Dad answered. Then, silence.

"That's strange." I thought. "Dad's not talking and it's a phone call."

"Becky," Dad stated, his voice sad and a bit shaky, "You need to take this."

I could sense something was wrong and listened from the door of my bedroom. Mom gasped. "What? No!!" She burst into tears and began to sob horribly.

I grew afraid. Something was terribly wrong and I knew it. What I did not know was that the world, as I knew it, had come to an end.

I froze in the doorway, afraid to do or ask anything. A few minutes later, Dad, arms around Mom, slowly walked up the stairs and into their bedroom where he helped her lie down. Her sobbing was uncontrollable. Dad walked back to my room, looked down and said, "John, Grandpa died tonight. Heart attack."

I was stunned. I had never known someone who died. Dad's parents had died before I was born. This was all new and very scary to me. I walked to my bed and sat on it, not knowing what to do or even how to feel.

Dad then returned to Mom to attempt to comfort her.

"Mommy, I'm sorry," I called out.

Through her sobs and tears of grief, she managed, "Thank you."

Dad walked back into to my room. "John, we'll be leaving for the mountains tomorrow morning. Try to sleep now. Everything will be okay."

"Okay, Daddy," I said, but somehow knew things were anything but okay.

"Oh my God in heaven!!" Mom mourned loudly. "I never forgave him and now… now… he's gone. I'll never have a chance to tell him I loved him. Oh my God, what have I done?" Mom's crying continued late into the night.

The next morning our family traveled to Grammy's house. The grown-ups visited, talked, and the children were kept busy in another room. The funeral came and went, but it was all a blur to me. All I remembered was visiting the funeral home and seeing Grandpa lying in the casket. I asked, "Mom, what is death?" Mom explained death was when the body stopped working and the spirit left it. I thought for a moment then asked, "Mommy, if I stuck Grandpa with a pin would he feel it?" Mom's eyes watered as she told me Grandpa would not feel it. At that point, Dad took me back to Grammy's house. Mom wanted to stay with Grandpa's body.

Over the next months, things began to change at home. Mom stayed in bed a lot. Dad began missing work to take her to doctor appointments. Instead of having delicious meals, Dad started cooking. Instead of nice meat, we ate SPAM or fried bologna. Instead of the corn and other vegetables Mom formerly canned, everything was from the store, and it just didn't taste the same.

Mom was not the same person I had always known. She and Dad began to argue a lot. Every day they would scream and yell at each other. Whenever this happened, I would go into my room, shut the door and sit, hoping they would not bring the fight into my room.

After some arguments, I noticed Dad would wince and grab his chest. I did not know why he did that, but one day Mom sat me down and stated, "John, your father has been suffering from chest pains. I think he may have a heart attack. Don't you ever do anything to upset him, because you could give him a heart attack. Understand?" She walked away, but I remained motionless, stunned and terrified. My heart began to race, my breathing quickened and I became dizzy and felt as if I would vomit. I knew I had to be perfect or Daddy would die and it would be my fault. Mom's words were a terrible burden on me.

My attendance at school remained good, but I would often sit in class hearing what the teacher was saying or looking at the pages in the book, but my mind, however, would often be on Dad, wondering if he would have a heart attack and die that day.

My grades dropped. The teacher approached me during class one day and in front of the entire class sternly stated, "John, your grades have dropped and there is no excuse for it! You are smart, but frankly, I think you're being lazy. I fully expect your grades to improve. Do you understand me young man?" I could feel my face blushing and felt as if every eye in the room was piercing through my body. I tried to concentrate better, but Mom's warning kept roaring through my mind.

At home, I never mentioned the incident to my parents because I knew it would upset Dad. I kept it all inside. I often kept unpleasant things inside so my father would not die.

"John, sit down," Dad stated one afternoon after I arrived home from school. "Your mother is going to see a psychiatrist. She needs help."

"What's a psychiatrist?"

"A doctor who specializes in helping people like your mother."

"And, we're going to have to cut back on some things. The doctor bills are piling up and we have to give up some things."

"Like what?"

"I'm not sure yet. We'll have to see. I sold my half of the hardware store to Brady today."

"You don't have a job?"

"I still have a job. I'll still be at the store, and Brady told me he would not partner with anyone else. He said when I get the money, he'll sell half of it back to me."

"That's nice."

"Yes, it is. Brady's a good friend. But we won't have as much money as usual, so things will be tight for a while."

"How long?"

"Not sure, son."

"What about all the money you got from Mr. Frederick?"

"It's all going to doctors. All of it and then some. But don't you worry. We'll be alright."

I was sad and mourning the life I once had, but knew to stay quiet and pretend all was fine so my Dad would not become upset.

The next day I learned about a new medicine Mom would be taking. Darvon. I had no idea what Darvon was, but I hoped it would make Mom well. Mom began taking it, but she would only stagger around the house. Her eyes would roll back in her head, her speech would become slurred and she would stumble into walls and doors. When Mom took Darvon, I tried to avoid her. Sometimes it worked, sometimes it didn't. I learned very quickly to hate Darvon. It was only making things worse.

But not all days were bad. At times, I would hear the vacuum cleaner running. The sound of the vacuum cleaner was comforting to me, as I knew if it was running, Mom hadn't taken a Darvon and she would be okay to be around. Those days, however, were few and far between.

Tuesdays were always busy at the hardware store and Dad usually worked late. Even though it was still daylight outside, Mom was asleep after taking Darvon. I tried to ignore it. I stayed in my room and worked on some math homework. I was almost finished when I heard Mom staggering around her bedroom. I quickly closed my bedroom door and tried to finish my homework, but all I could concentrate on was Mom bumping into things, and I could hear objects hitting the floor as she leaned on furniture to steady herself. I sat in my room, wishing Mom would stop it. I then heard the door to her bedroom swing open and Mom slam into it, knocking it hard against a sliding closet door. I froze. I could hear what sounded like her falling down. I remained motionless, afraid to move.

Speech slurred, Mom called out, "John!" But I did not move. She called me several more times, but I was frozen with fear and could not think of what to do.

"John, get in here now!" Mom screamed. The screaming startled me. I got up, slowly opened my bedroom door and looked across the hall, where my mother was on her side and trying to get off the floor with no success.

"Get over here and help me up!" she ordered. I angrily walked over, grabbed her arm and tried to lift her, but she was far too heavy and virtually unable to help herself. After several minutes, I managed to help her to the edge of the bed, where she dragged herself back onto it and passed out.

I was furious. I ran into my bedroom, grabbed my football, ran outside to the back yard and repeatedly punted from one end of the yard to the other. The more I thought about what had just happened the harder I kicked. I kicked and kicked until the sweat streaming down my face covered the tears of hurt and anger that flowed from my eyes. Not even Droopy or Garfunkel could help me feel better. I continued until I saw Dad drive up. I did not want to give Dad a heart attack, but the pain inside me overpowered my worries and I ran as fast as he could to him.

"Dad!" I begged, "Please make Mom stop taking Darvon."

"The doctor says it will help her."

"It's not! All she does is stumble around! She even fell down when you weren't here and kept yelling at me to get her up. I couldn't lift her. All I could do was drag her back up into bed and then she passed out again and drooled all over the place. Dad, make her stop!"

Dad's shoulders slumped and he looked hopeless. "I'll do what I can." Dad did not appear angry, but I followed him around for the next hour or so just to make sure he would not have a heart attack.

I also began to withdraw from my friends. I totally stopped having friends over because I was ashamed of what Mom might do. At recess I walked around, alone, head down, not really thinking about anything. Just slowly walking. It was a sad, lonely time for me, and no one at school seemed to notice. If they did, they did not care, for no one spoke to me or did anything to show they cared. I felt completely alone and worthless.

Mom became more and more withdrawn. She told Dad and me that if we ever called her, to let the phone ring twice, hang up and then call again. Otherwise, she told us, she would never answer the phone.

One sunny day at school, some kids were playing kickball. I was walking far off to the side away from everyone, when someone yelled, "Heads up!" I turned around just as the ball hit at my feet. It took an awkward bounce and hit my right pinky finger hard and I immediately knew my finger was broken. I grabbed my finger, kicked the ball back toward those playing, walked to the teacher and told her what had happened. "Go run hot water on it. We'll be in later," she replied. The hot water only made it hurt worse. When everybody came back inside the teacher sent me to the school clinic.

Two nice moms were in the clinic. Students' moms always operated the clinic, as the school had no money to pay a nurse to do the job. They immediately put ice on the broken finger and spoke very sweetly to me. My soul ached for my Mom to be like these ladies, but I knew better. The ladies told me to call home. I dialed the number, let it ring two times and hung up. Before I could start dialing again, one of the ladies asked me why I had hung up.

"I think it was a wrong number," I said, hoping they would believe me.

"No honey. You dialed the number on your emergency card," one lady calmly stated.

I felt embarrassed and could feel my face blushing. I knew I had to tell them the truth. Feeling ashamed, I looked down at the floor and quietly stated, "My Mom says we have to let it ring two times, hang up and call again or she won't answer." The ladies looked at one another.

"Okay, sweetheart, dial it again."

I slowly dialed once more, hoping Mom would not have taken any Darvon. Mom answered and slurred, "Hello?"

"Mom, I broke my finger and …"

"What were you doing? This is just great! Now I'll have to call your father!!" Mom screamed and slammed the phone down.

I felt the familiar humiliation. I felt my face blush, my heart pound, my breathing speeding, but I dared not look up. I stood motionless and stared at the floor.

The ladies easily overheard mom screaming at me and immediately comforted me and told me it was not my fault. They both seemed to be trying not to cry. *"Why are they crying?"* I thought. *"I'm the one with the busted finger."*

About thirty minutes later the clinic phone rang. One of the moms answered it, listened, and then said, "Right away." Turning to me, she kindly said, "Your father is in the office to pick you up, sweetheart." Dad had arrived to take me to the doctor's office. He was not upset with me, so I knew he would not have a heart attack. After an hour or so at the doctor's office it was confirmed my finger was indeed broken in two places and a splint was put on it.

I was angry at my Mom and did not want to see her. I told Dad about the phone call and the clinic ladies crying. Dad's jaw clenched, his knuckles turning white as he seemed to be crushing the steering wheel, he began breathing harder and he stared straight ahead, saying nothing. When I saw his reaction, I became very tense and looked straight ahead, worrying about his heart and what would happen once we got home. Neither Dad nor I spoke the rest of the way home.

Dad stormed into the master bedroom, slammed the door and ordered Mom to get up. "I can count the number of times you've smiled in the past two years on one hand!" he yelled. "But now you've humiliated our entire family! You're going to Vanderbilt Hospital, like it or not!" A screaming fight that seemed to last forever ensued. I sat motionless in my room, every angry word piercing my soul.

Two weeks later, Dad's cousin, Aunt Amy, arrived from the Boundary. Aunt Amy was a kind, gentle woman who always made me feel welcome when she visited. She was Logan's mother. Logan was my favorite cousin. I had no brothers or sisters and I considered Logan more of a brother than a cousin. "John," Dad stated, "Aunt Amy is going to take care of you for a few days while I take Mommy to Nashville. She is going to see some doctors and hopefully she will start to get well."

"Fine." I said. I didn't believe my mom would ever be better and I was terribly sad. In fact, I had given up on the idea of ever being happy again.

I liked Aunt Amy. She was a rather short, slim woman with long dark brown hair and hazel eyes. She was an excellent cook and she always spoke softly. Her quiet manner was comforting to me, as I was so tired of all the yelling I had heard over the past couple of years.

Dad came back home two days later. "Your mother is in good hands, John. Aunt Amy has agreed to stay here until she can come home."

"When will that be?" I cautiously asked.

"I'm not sure. Maybe three or four weeks. Maybe longer."

"Weeks?" I exclaimed.

"Yes, son. Weeks," Dad said.

The weeks passed and I grew used to having Aunt Amy around. No one screamed at each other, the food was much better than Dad's cooking and I began to relax. I also began to have friends over once again and was not as withdrawn at school as before. I worried about Mom, but in the back of my mind I worried even more about what would happen when she returned. Would she go back to taking medicine? Would she get even worse and start hitting? I felt confused and helpless.

"John, I have some good news for you. I will leave tomorrow morning to bring your mother back from Nashville," Dad said.

I immediately tensed up and asked in a shaking voice, "Will she be better, Dad?"

"Yes. The doctors say she is ready to come home."

"And be nice? What about the Darvon?"

"No more Darvon."

I breathed a huge sigh of relief and smiled at Dad and Aunt Amy. It felt good to smile, something I had not done in many months.

"Where has Mom been for so long anyway?"

Dad looked down, paused for a moment and told me that she had been at Vanderbilt Hospital in Nashville.

Two days later Mom and Dad arrived home. I was uneasy about seeing her. I feared she was not well or that she would go back to Darvon.

I heard the car pull up and Aunt Amy called for me to come down. I froze, not knowing what to do or expect. I sat on the edge of my bed for a minute. Part of me wanted to go downstairs, but part wanted to run off and hide. I knew I had to go downstairs. I very slowly and tentatively walked out of my room. I stopped at the top of the stairs, afraid to go on.

"John!" Aunt Amy called. "Hurry up, sweetheart. Your folks are home!"

I took one step at a time, stopping on each stair, my heart pounding, breathing heavy and palms sweating. I very slowly made it down the stairs, but then turned to run back to my room.

"Oh, John," Aunt Amy softly said as she put her arm around my shaking shoulders, "It's okay to be nervous. Will you trust me?"

Still avoiding looking toward the front door I nodded my head yes. Aunt Amy took my hand and helped me walk out of the house. I continued looking down as if avoiding a terrible, unseen force that would cause me harm.

Mom got out of the car, stood straight, walked to me, hugged me and said, "I love you John. I know I was hard to live with. I will try to be better now. It won't be easy, but I will make it." And for the first time in more than two years, she smiled at me.

As the days and weeks went on, Mom stayed free of Darvon. The reassuring hum of the vacuum cleaner became commonplace and the smell of freshly cooked cornbread and beans regularly filled the home once again. I no longer remained withdrawn and the screaming arguments ceased. Mom, Dad and I were at long last a family once more.

CHAPTER 9

THE RAMBLER
AND THE
PRINCESS

D ad drove a used 1964 American Motors Rambler. It had a green body and a white roof. The steering wheel was huge, the metal dashboard was a faded green, the radio never worked and when it rained the car would not even start. But none of that mattered to me. I liked the Rambler. The seats were very comfortable and the front seats would recline all the way back until they rested on the back seat. I enjoyed lowering the seats and then bouncing around the interior of the car.

"Becky, where's John?" Dad asked.

"I believe he's outside," she replied.

"Okay. Thanks. I'll find him."

Dad walked outside, carrying a toolbox and a small cardboard box with a new distributor cap and spark plugs inside. He called for me but I could not hear him. Dad walked around to the side of the house. "Should have known," he laughed.

Appearing to Dad momentarily, and then disappearing, again and again, I was bouncing around the interior of the Rambler.

Dad knocked on a window and opened a door. "John, stop that. You'll ruin the seats."

"Promise I won't. Besides, this is fun!"

"You'll hit your head on something and get hurt."

"I won't."

"Out now, John. I need your help."

"What with?"

Dad had said the Rambler needed a new distributor cap, whatever that was. He had told me that the old one had a crack in it and that was why the car never started when it rained. He was going to install new spark plugs, too. He raised the hood and began removing the old spark plugs and distributor.

"Hand me that wrench," Dad stated.

As I handed Dad the tool, I was thinking and asked, "Dad, lots of kids keep telling me their great-grandmothers were Cherokee princesses. What's with that?"

"Dad chuckled as he worked on a rusty screw. "Just ignore it, John. No tribe ever had princesses."

"Then why do people keep saying it? Are they stupid?"

"There! Got it!" Dad delighted as he successfully removed the screw. "They aren't stupid, son, just misguided."

"Mis…what?"

"I've heard that nonsense from wannabees all my life. Used to make me mad. Then I tried explaining why they were wrong, but that only made people mad. So just ignore it, or say something like, 'That's interesting.'"

"What's a wannabee?" I asked.

Dad put the tool down, paused a moment and explained. "Wannabee is a word that means 'want to be.' You see, lots of white people want to be Indian. Most of them think they're Cherokee. They really cause problems for real Cherokees."

"Real Cherokees. You mean enrolled?"

Dad thought for a moment and said, "Enrolled means you're an official member of the tribe."

"But we're not enrolled. Does that make us wannabees?"

"No John. We certainly are not wannabees."

"How do you know?"

"First of all, look in a mirror, son. Also, our family is on the old rolls."

"Rolls?"

"Official lists of tribal members. And, do we ever go around playing Indian?"

Laughing, I said, "Of course not!"

"Do we have the culture?"

"Yes, I think so."

"Good. Remember, you are Cherokee first, American second. Always remember that."

"I will."

Dad removed the old distributor cap and looked very carefully at it. "Look there. There's the crack."

"That's tiny. That little crack let water in?"

"Guess so. Hand me that box."

I picked up the box with the new distributor cap inside. Dad popped it open, took out the new distributor cap and started to install it.

"So, why do so many white people think they're part Cherokee, Dad? And if they're not, why would they want to be?"

As Dad continued working on the Rambler, he said, "Look, John. I've told you before. There are only three real groups of Cherokees. What are they?"

I rolled my eyes, placed my hands on my hips, made a very serious face, and in a voice that attempted to sound like Dad's, I proclaimed, "The Eastern Band of Cherokee Indians, The Cherokee Nation of Oklahoma and the United Keetoowah Band."

Trying not to laugh, Dad looked at me and shook his head. I had made my point. No more reminders needed. "Right. Lots of people have stories, but they don't have the culture, the language, a land base or anything else. They honestly believe they are part Cherokee. Sometimes they even get together and call themselves this or that Cherokee Tribe, but they're not recognized."

"Recognized?"

"The BIA will never consider them to be real Cherokee tribes because they have no evidence they were ever part of the tribe."

"BIA?" I asked.

"Means Boss Indians Around," Dad quipped.

"Huh?"

"Not really. BIA stands for the Bureau of Indian Affairs."

"What do they do?"

Dad thought for a moment, and then stated with a straight face, "They boss Indians around."

"Oh never mind," I said, knowing Dad was being silly.

I paused to think, then asked, "Dad, why would people want to make fake tribes?"

"I don't know. Like I said, they don't have the history, culture, language…"

"Hey! You won't teach me the language."

"That's for your own good."

"How's that good?"

"I'm not getting into it. Trust me. If you spoke the language at school it would be bad for you."

"I won't speak it at school."

Dad laid the tools down, looked at me and explained, "You would, just like I did. Every time I spoke it, I got into trouble. Real trouble. One teacher I had used to pop me on top of my head with the end of her walking stick. I had knots on my head all the time, not to mention headaches. And, that was just for starters, John. I won't allow you to go through that. It's for your own good. Trust me."

"Alright," I said in a disappointed voice. I felt very disappointed Dad would not teach me the language. I knew a few words I had heard from people on the Boundary, but I could not carry on a conversation. I worried I would be ridiculed on the Boundary when people knew I could only speak English. Also, I felt irritated at Dad, because he always said, "English is the most commonly spoken foreign language in North America," but then only let me learn English, not Cherokee.

Then, after quietly thinking, my face became very serious, I looked at Dad, who was

once again working on the car, and stated, "I wish all those white people would think they're Choctaw or something," I angrily pouted.

Dad burst into laughter, the wrench slipped and he smashed his fingers. "Dang it, John! Don't make me laugh when I'm under the hood."

I wasn't sure what was so funny, but after several minutes Dad got the new distributor cap and spark plugs installed.

"There, now. Next time it rains we'll see if it'll start."

"What about the radio?"

"Forget the radio. I just want it to run," Dad chuckled.

Dad started the car. "Sounds good!" Then he turned it off.

"Can I play in it now?" I asked.

"No. It's time for supper. Let's go inside and wash our hands."

"Okay," I said, slightly disappointed, but not surprised.

We walked into the house for supper.

CHAPTER 10

FOURTH GRADE

B y the time I was in fourth grade, Scotty's parents had divorced and he had moved away with his mother. I was in Mrs. Luca's class, was making good grades and was starting to make new friends.

I never meant to cause trouble, but I had heard some things at home about American history and I repeated them in class. I also remembered the times Grandpa had warned me not to believe everything the schools would try to teach about American history. I felt angry the school textbooks and teachers would lie about history, because lying was wrong. I also felt apprehensive because Grandpa had warned me the history classes would try to make Indians the bad guys, or look stupid in other ways, and I worried the other kids would make fun of me. I knew Grandpa would be proud of me if I spoke up in school and told the truth. I missed Grandpa and decided to honor him by telling the truth.

One afternoon in social studies, Mrs. Luca was trying to explain the symbolism of the American flag to the class.

"Who can tell me what the fifty stars represent? John?"

"My grandpa said they each represent a state the white people stole."

"Out into the hall! Now!" Mrs. Luca barked. I complied but had no idea why she had become angry.

Another day Mrs. Luca stated, "George Washington is the father of our country."

"He must have had a lot of kids," I whispered to a friend.

"Yes, John? Would you care to explain it to the entire class?" asked Mrs. Luca. "I'll try. My dad says he was really smart but that he would do really bad things with any woman he could get his hands on . . . no wait. That was Benjamin Franklin." Hallway again.

Later was the story of Sacajawea. "Can anyone tell us about this brave Indian princess?" asked Mrs. Luca. I blurted out, "There were no such things and Indian princesses. My dad says that's a white man's fairy tale. And he says Sacajawea should have got Lewis and Clark lost and just left them." This time I had to stand in the corner.

Later came the day when Mrs. Luca began teaching about Andrew Jackson. "Who can tell us something about Andrew Jackson?" she asked.

"I can." I answered. "I know one of his parent's names!"

"Really? And what would that be?"

"Bitch!" I said proudly.

"What?" Mrs. Luca gasped, her mouth hanging open.

"Yeah. Every time somebody starts talking about Andrew Jackson, my dad says 'He was a son of…'"

"Stop right there!" Mrs. Luca angrily barked. "We'll see what the principal has to say about this."

Mr. Shepherd, the assistant principal, was a tall, heavy man with a scraggly, grey beard who spoke slowly and often changed subjects in the middle of his sentences. He never seemed to leave his office and word had it he actually lived in a secret room in the school. Mr. Shepherd's office was small. It had a desk, a couple of file cabinets and three old chairs against the wall. It was dimly lit, and a door was in the corner. It looked like a closet door, but all the kids had heard it was a secret room that only Mr. Shepherd was allowed to enter.

"Young man," Mr. Shepherd drawled, "I understand you have been causing problems in class."

"I wasn't trying to," I said as my voice trembled. I had heard Mr. Shepherd had an electric paddle. Kids said he would make you bend over, push the button and a machine would paddle you till you bled. I looked around the room but did not see it. *"He must have it hidden,"* I surmised.

Mr. Shepherd paused, stared into my face, stroked his scruffy, grey beard, then slowly said, "Mrs. Luca tells me you made fun of the flag, said disparaging things about Lewis and Clark, and that you said something dreadful about Andrew Jackson."

"You cannot badmouth our heroes." stated Mr. Shepherd.

I thought, *"Heroes? They're not heroes."* But I dared not upset the principal.

"Do you read your history book?"

"Yes, sir," I quietly said as I looked down at my feet.

"Did you read about any Indian heroes? No. And do you know why? Because, there were none."

Immediately I thought of Dragging Canoe, Corn Tassel, Sequoyah, Junaluska, Yonaguska, Oconastota and other heroes my Dad and Grandpa had told me about.

Mr. Shepherd continued. "You see, you people needed us to come over here and bring civilization. Read any history book. The Indians thought the white men were gods."

"That's a lie," I thought. *"Dad says the white men were violent and hairy and that they made everybody sick and tons of people died."* But again,

I dared not speak.   "The white man discovered America. Indians discovered nothing. That should tell you who was more advanced. Besides, when the white man arrived, the Indians were sitting on top of many precious resources, but they weren't doing anything with them. They were living in the Stone Age. And think, the white man arrived and in only a few hundred years built the greatest country in the history of the world."

At this point I was numb. I could think of nothing and was hearing nothing Mr. Shepherd was saying. I was embarrassed, intimidated and angry, but could only sit, head down, arms folded and take it.

"Are you listening to me?" Mr. Shepherd loudly asked.

"Yes."

"Will there be any more trouble?"

"No."

"Very well. Return to class. And I do not expect to see your face in here again."

With head down and spirit broken, I slowly left the office. I did not return to class. I slowly walked to the restroom, entered a stall, closed the door, sat down and silently wept.

CHAPTER 11

FIFTH GRADE HISTORY

I was in fifth grade and was in Mrs. Jameson's class. Mrs. Jameson was a tall, thin white woman who wore large glasses with a chain on the stems of her glasses that wrapped around the back of her neck. Good thing too, because her glasses kept sliding off her nose. Class started off slowly and my mind recalled the dream. Then it all seemed to fit. "*Mrs. Jameson always was so nice to the blonde-haired kids, not so nice to the other white kids and she doesn't like me at all,*" I thought. "*Whenever I raise my hand to answer a question, she never calls on me, but if I don't raise my hand, she always calls on me and then makes fun of my answer when I get it wrong.*" I mentioned it to my friend, Wade, who sat next to me, and Wade said it was because Mrs. Jameson hated me. He said, "Watch. I'll raise my hand and she'll call on me if your hand is up too." We tried it and sure enough she called on Wade. Then Wade whispered to me, "I'll raise my hand but keep yours down." We did, and she called on me and then made fun of my answer. Wade said, "You need to raise your hand when you don't know the answer but keep it down if you do." It worked for a day or two but then Mrs. Jameson caught on and moved me to the back of the room and away from all my friends.

The school was overcrowded and everyone had to walk to the cafeteria, get their lunches, and go back and eat in the classroom. I knew I was different. The other kids had little noses that turned up. They were always sticking spoons on their noses and the spoons would stay. I tried it, but the spoon always slid off. My nose was too pointy. It was embarrassing.

Mrs. Jameson never seemed to notice anyone putting spoons on their noses, but the time or two I tried it she scolded me. She said I was being uncivilized. "They do it too…"

"I will not argue with you, young man!" exclaimed Mrs. Jameson, and I never tried to put a spoon on my nose again.

Social Studies started again after lunch and the class was reading from a book called <u>Your Country and Mine: Our American Neighbors</u>. It had a yellow cover with a picture of white mountain men and an Indian woman with a baby standing behind them. The first chapters kept stating Indians thought all the white men were gods. This day the class was on page ninety-nine and the title of the chapter was "The Pioneers on the March." The school only had one book for every four students so we sat in groups and rotated the book when it was one's turn to read. The chapter said Daniel Boone discovered Kentucky. It said some Indians tried to kill him but he was faster and stronger and got away. A drawing showed Boone jumping off a cliff and getting away from Indians. The caption of the picture was, "Daniel Boone escaped!" I raised my hand. Mrs. Jameson ignored me, so I shook my hand around.

"John, what is it?"

"This picture is all wrong."

"Really? Why don't you explain it to us?"

"First of all, no Indians ever dressed like that. Besides, if they really wanted to kill Boone they would just shoot him, not chase him with axes. And, look at Boone. He's jumping off a cliff at a dead tree. Those limbs would break and he'd fall all the way to…"

"Enough! It would not be in the book if it weren't true," Mrs. Jameson snorted.

Most of the other kids laughed. Some looked at me and shook their heads in disgust. I was badly embarrassed and decided to never speak up again in class.

I remained silent in class for several months until it was time to study Canada. On page 390 it told a story about the Mounties and some Indians. The book stated, "The Indians complained that the railroad would frighten away the buffalo and ruin their hunting grounds. Often they tried to drive workmen off the job.

For example, a large band of Indians galloped up to the railroad workmen, shrieking and whooping. 'Red man hate white man's steam horse!' shouted their chief. 'Leave our hunting grounds.'

Then the Indians slid from their ponies. They set up teepees on the new track and shot arrows into the air.

The workmen fled in terror but soon they returned. Mounties stationed nearby had rushed to the scene to take command.

The Mountie leader spoke sternly to the chief. 'Take your teepees down and move on!' he ordered. 'This railroad must be built!'

'No! We stay!' declared the chief.

'Leave here at once!' commanded the Mountie. 'I shall give you just fifteen minutes to move your belongings!'

Still the Indians paid no attention to the order. Therefore, when the time was up, the Mountie marched to the chief's teepee and jerked its heavy buffalo hide to the ground. Then he pulled down another teepee and another.

The Indians were astonished at such courage. Because this leader was fearless and meant business, they gave in. Grumbling, they gathered up their things and left. The Mountie had won this battle without firing a single shot, and the railroad building continued."

Without realizing it, I proclaimed, "This is stupid!"

"Instantly, other students yelled, "No, you're stupid!" and "Indians are stupid!" A couple of paper wads, one from in front, and one from the side hit me.

"Settle down, class," Mrs. Jameson calmly stated. "Indians weren't necessarily stupid. They of course were obviously not as advanced as white people. They just needed us to come over here and teach them how to be good civilized, Christian people. Not only did the white man civilize the Indians, we actually gave them free land to live on. None of us gets free land, do we children?" She stared at me the entire time she spoke. Most of the white kids replied, "No, Mrs. Jameson." A few laughed, but some, mainly the nice girls looked at me with sympathy.

I was furious and embarrassed at the same time. I looked down toward my desk and did not look up again. I also never said another word in social studies the entire year. My grades also went from A to C. I knew my Dad had told me how the white invaders had stolen the land and killed so many people. I knew about the Trail of Tears and the reservation system, what Dad called prisoner of war camps. But, I knew not to mention any of this at home, because I knew with dad's temper, he would tear the school apart. I had to protect my Dad, so I never said a word.

The old recurring dream of not belonging began invading my sleep once again.

CHAPTER 12

THE BULLYING

ixth grade began and I was one of the smaller boys in the class, standing 4' 6" tall and weighing 84 pounds. I had no problems during school, but things were about to take a very ominous turn at the bus stop. Several new families had moved into the neighborhood and three of them had very large, mean boys in eighth grade who were trouble makers. Ken Smith, Sam Trotsky and Felix Porter were known trouble. They were notorious for vandalizing houses and cars, slashing tires and smashing mailboxes. They had been arrested several times for shoplifting and attempting to steal beer from local stores. They never targeted my house because Garfunkel always chased them off. They also learned Dad had been a sergeant in the 101st Airborne, so they stayed clear of our house. The bus stop was a different story.

I barely came up to their chests and the three of them decided to target me. At times they spit on me, kicked and punched me, choked me as they laughed as I could not breathe and would trip me and sometimes even throw rocks at me.

One day after a night of heavy rain, Sam grabbed me from behind and with help from Ken, picked me up and threw me face down in mud. I had quick reflexes and landed on my forearms and knees and my forehead hit the mud. When I arrived at school the teacher asked what had happened. I told her I had tripped and fallen into some mud. She sent me to the clinic to get cleaned up. A nice mother was in the clinic. She had me give her my shirt and she rinsed off the mud from the elbows and the splatters of mud off the front of the shirt and then dried it as much as possible. While she did that, I rinsed the mud out of my hair and off my forehead. The nice lady gave me a small towel to dry my face and hair, then wiped as much mud off the knees of my pants as possible and then returned the shirt to me. I put my shirt back on and thanked the nice lady. She told me to be more careful in the future.

On another day, Felix held me from behind while the other two punched and kicked me in the stomach and chest until I doubled over in pain. I never spoke to anyone about this attack because I was embarrassed.

On yet another occasion, Sam grabbed me by the throat and choked me so hard I could not breathe. When I was almost ready to pass out, the other two grabbed me and threw me down backward onto the hard, cracked ground behind a large bush that stood next to the road. My head struck the earth with such force my head bounced off it. I could then hear voices, but they sounded like distant echoes. I tried to get up, but my body did not respond. I then heard a muffled thud next to my head but I could not understand what it was and was unable to turn my head to see what it was. At that point everything faded to darkness and I lost consciousness.

What seemed to be the next moment, the hot sun awoke me. My head throbbed in pain and I slowly sat up behind the large bush. My book bag was next to my head, but all the other kids were gone and the sun was much farther up in the sky than I last remembered. I then realized the bullies had knocked me out and everyone had left me. Rubbing the painful back of my head, I very slowly rose to my feet, picked up my book bag and very slowly walked home.

Upon arriving home, I discovered both the front and carport doors were locked. Droopy and Garfunkel began barking and jumping up to see me, so I walked to the fence gate and entered the back yard where I momentarily patted each dog. I walked to the laundry room door and found it unlocked, so I went inside and made my way to my bedroom. Mom was asleep, so I changed clothes, laid down on my bed and fell asleep. A few hours later I awoke and my head felt somewhat better. I quietly went to the kitchen to get something to eat, hoping not to wake up Mom. I began to eat, but it made me feel like throwing up, so I returned to my bedroom and stayed in bed until the headache subsided.

Mom slept past the time I normally arrived home from school and Dad arrived home around 6:00. Ashamed and not wanting to upset my parents, I said nothing about the day's happenings.

The following morning at the bus stop, no one spoke to me. In fact, they did not even make eye contact with me. Even the bullies kept their distance, huddling together and occasionally glancing in my direction.

When I arrived in homeroom, I told the teacher I had felt sick the day before and she marked it down as an excused absence in her large grade book.

Don Greene, who had been best friends with me only a few years prior, was the cool kid in school. He was a year older than I was and was very tall and strong for his age. All he would have had to do was tell the bullies to stop and the bullying would have ceased, but he merely stood by and watched. I felt betrayed by Don and the pain of being betrayed was as bad as any physical pain inflicted by the bullies.

I finally complained to my parents, but Mom had recently begun taking Darvon again and Dad's temper was white hot. "Get tough!" Dad would yell at me.

"They're all way bigger than me! They outnumber me and if I start to take one on the others come after me. I can't beat them!" I exclaimed.

"Take out the ringleader! The others will back away," demanded Dad.

"I can't reach their faces and besides, there isn't a ringleader. They are all just as mean as the others! Do something, Dad!" I implored.

About that time Mom stumbled and fell.

"Later," Dad angrily said as he left to get Mom back into bed.

The torment lasted the entire school year. Another time, Sam hit me so hard it split my skin open over my left cheek bone and blood poured out. The bullies laughed, yelled racial slurs at me and tripped me as I started to head back home because of all the blood on my shirt. "E v e r y b o d y knows your mom's a damn drunk." yelled Ken as Felix and Sam laughed and howled as I slowly made my way back home.

"What did you do?" demanded Mom as I entered the house.

"Sam Trotsky hit me. I have to change shirts."

"You need stitches!" Dad growled. "What will it take for you to stand up for yourself?"

Exasperated, I exploded, "Do you know what they call me in Chorus? 3-T and it means teeny tiny tenor! When we lined up shortest to tallest on picture day, I was the first one in line, even ahead of the girls, and you expect me to beat up three huge, mean eighth graders?"

I missed the first half day of school getting stitches. Dad then dropped me off at school around lunch time and all the other children wanted to know what happened. I just ignored their inquiries.

I again withdrew, but now felt angry, alone and hopeless. The only peace I knew was with my dogs or when I was asleep, unless the recurring dream of not belonging raised its ugly head. Breakfast became a thing of the past as Mom was always asleep and Dad had started leaving early for work.

Near the end of the school year, I was walking to the bus after school one afternoon when Rob Murphy, a friend of the three bullies stuck his head out the window and spit a huge glob on my head.

"Got him right on the head!" laughed Murphy. "Hell yeah!" laughed the others.

"Hey chief! How do you like that?" yelled Murphy.

Knowing I was helpless to retaliate, I sat alone in the front of the bus, got off at my stop as quickly as possible and ran home to wash my hair. I dared not tell my parents lest they yell at me again.

I considered telling the adults at school about the endless bullying, but I had heard the adults only talked to the bullies but did nothing to stop them. I heard the bullying would become worse if I spoke up when the adults took no real action, so I said nothing to them. I knew when the adults only talked to bullies, nothing would change.

The school year ended, the bullies were headed for high school and I finally felt a bit of relief. The relief was accompanied by resentment towards my parents for never helping me. During this time in my life, Droopy and Garfunkel were my main comfort, as they loved me unconditionally and played with me any time I went into the back yard. Droopy and Garfunkel sensed a deep sadness in me and often curled up at my feet. I would pet them and wonder how I could ever survive without my beloved dogs.

CHAPTER 13

THE PEA CREEK REDNECKS

Pea Creek Elementary School was about five miles south of my school, Maple Ridge Middle. Maple Ridge had been for grades one through eight, but the school system built a new primary school for grades one through five and the school I had always attended was renamed Maple Ridge Middle School and was for grades six through eight. Every year students from Pea Creek would move to Maple Ridge. They caused fights, were always in the lowest groups of every class and caused trouble everywhere they went.

That year, my class got the worst of the Pea Creek rednecks. The two meanest were Neal Humphrey and Norman Kidd. They were both at least a year older than the rest of the students, as they had each failed at least one grade. They were much bigger than any other kids, Humphrey being larger than Kidd, and they always smelled like cigarette smoke. They never seemed to wash, their hair was always greasy and messy and they never brushed their teeth. If either of them was in the restroom nobody else dared enter. The same was true with the water fountains. If they were getting water the rest of the kids stayed away. Humphrey and Kidd enjoyed intimidating the other students, and even a couple of teachers.

In language arts class, the teacher brought in job applications to teach the class how to fill out such forms and also, she said, to start thinking about our futures. On my application I wrote down I was going to be a National Park Ranger and make a whopping $10,000 a year. All of my friends had good ideas such as doctors, scientists, engineers, artists, and so on.

Humphrey and Kidd also worked together and it appeared that for the first time ever they were actually doing school work. Mrs. Rose, the language arts teacher also seemed pleasantly surprised. After a while she took the applications up and began reading them to the class and commenting not only on students' career aspirations, but also how correctly each had completed the forms. When she came across Kidd's and Humphrey's applications her face turned red, she clenched her jaw and her eyes became large with anger. Both Kidd and Humphrey began laughing hysterically and slapping each other fiercely. She ordered both of them into the hall. Everyone else left in the room strained to hear what they could. It turned out both of them put down they were going to be in prison; Humphrey for robbing banks and Kidd for stealing cars and kidnapping beautiful women. My friends and I laughed, not because the rednecks were funny, but because Kidd and Humphrey probably would actually end up in prison.

After gym was over one day, everybody was changing clothes in the locker room. The locker room was an open room with wooden benches along the walls. A large room with multiple shower heads was where everyone was supposed to shower after gym class, and the locker room had one toilet and a sink. The locker room was always crowded, steamy and smelly. Without really thinking, I looked up and across the locker room saw Humphrey, and said, "Humphrey Dumphrey." Although I thought I had whispered it, Neal Humphrey heard me.

"I'm gonna kick your ass!" yelled Humphrey.

"No. No you're not," I replied.

"Oh yeah? Why not?"

"Cause you can't catch me!" I yelled as I dashed out the locker room door. I was one of the smallest boys but I was a very fast runner. Neal Humphrey, on the other hand, was very big, but slow.

As I made it to the gym door, Humphrey came barreling out of the locker room yelling, "Come back here! I'm gonna kill you!"

I ran through the gym doors and turned right to run down the hall, but it was blocked by a huge group of big eighth graders walking toward the library. After reversing direction I barely missed getting grabbed by Humphrey as I again ran by the gym doors after reversing direction.

"You've had it!" Humphrey yelled as he gave chase.

I reached a set of stairs. I ran up the stairs as fast as I could because if Humphrey caught me, I knew I would get broken in half. I reached the upstairs hallway and ran toward the science class, which was the next class and was taught by Mrs. Phillips, a large woman who was not afraid of the rednecks. As I ran past the cafeteria, I paused to look back to see where Humphrey was. Humphrey had just made it to the top of the stairs and was out of breath, bent over with his huge hands on his knees. Feeling impish, I grinned and decided to have some fun. Humphrey was out of breath and even though he was trying to yell, he was never going to catch me.

I ran about twenty feet and stopped, acting like I was winded. As soon as Humphrey came within a few seconds of catching me, I would take off again. I kept it up all the way down the hall and Humphrey never figured out I was playing cat and mouse. Finally, I ran to the science room doorway and stopped. Humphrey was madder than ever and charging with all his might. I then calmly and slowly entered the room and made a sharp turn to the left and kept walking to my desk, where I sat down, opened my science book and acted as if nothing was happening. Mrs. Phillips was standing in front of her desk, which was located just inside the door to the right.

"I'm gonna kick your ass!" Humphrey screamed as he charged full speed through the door, smashing directly into Mrs. Phillips and knocking the book from her hands and scattering papers everywhere.

"Neal Humphrey!" yelled Mrs. Phillips, "How dare you! What is the meaning of this?! Out! Out in the hall immediately! You are in deep trouble now!" Humphrey stood there speechless, staring into space. I worked hard not to smile or laugh.

The day after Humphrey ran into Mrs. Phillips, the teachers announced they needed to find out what everyone's father did for a living. Several kids' fathers were doctors, engineers, or other jobs that paid a lot of money. When the teacher called on me, I said my dad worked at Frederick Hardware. The rednecks burst into laughter.

"Your dad don't work at no hardware store. Indians don't use tools," one of them yelled as the others began laughing.

"And your dad ain't even Indian. I seen him driving a car. Indians ride horses." Again, laughter from the rednecks.

"Hey, Chief! Where's your teepee?" taunted another.

I wanted so badly to respond, but the rednecks were bigger, meaner and they outnumbered me. I wanted the teacher to shut them up, which she finally did, but not before I was humiliated once again. I never understood why some teachers allowed the rednecks to get away with so much, but was glad I was a fast runner so they would never catch me.

CHAPTER 14

SQUID

Dealing with the Pea Creek rednecks was bad enough, but after Christmas break came even worse news…a new kid. He was an eighth grader from South Dakota who was supposed to be really mean. Nobody knew his real name, but his nickname was Squid.

My friends and I had spotted Squid from a distance. Squid was strong looking, pale with blonde hair. He put some kind of goo in his hair and made it stick straight up toward the sky. His glasses were black plastic frames with extremely thick round lenses that made his eyes look huge, so he actually looked like a squid. And he wore old cowboy boots.

My friends and I talked about ways to keep from getting caught by Squid. My best friends were Wade and Stephen. Stephen was very smart. His dad was a doctor and his mother was a nurse. Stephen had blonde wavy hair and blue eyes. I enjoyed being around Stephen because Stephen was nice and smart and never looked down at me because my family was not rich. Wade had light red hair and blue eyes and was the clown in the group. He was never bad, but almost every day he would say or do something so funny the entire class would laugh, even the teachers. I enjoyed the laughter Wade brought.

"I heard he dunks your head in the toilet and flushes it," Wade said. All the boys moaned and shook their heads.

"Let's all walk together in a group," said Stephen.

"And don't make eye contact," I added.

We decided to stay away from Squid whenever possible. We even planned how to use different routes around the school to avoid him.

About the same time Squid came to the school, another kid, a sixth grader named Herman showed up. Herman was a little taller than me and kind of chubby. He had very pale skin and black hair and he was a sissy in the way he talked and walked. Herman was harmless, but annoying to the other students. He constantly paid fake compliments to teachers to try to get on their good side. Herman's mother even started coming to school to do work for the teachers, and she would sometimes show up with snacks for them. She would always go out of her way to remind the teachers of all of Herman's wonderful talents. My friends and I saw all of this as a way to get special treatment for Herman. With most teachers it worked. Herman was always picked to run errands, he got to pick his own desk instead of being assigned like everyone else, and even when he would do or say something that would get any other kid in trouble the teachers seemed to just let it go. None of the kids liked Herman or his mom.

One teacher, though, didn't buy it-Mrs. Austin. Mrs. Austin treated everybody equally bad. She disliked everyone; students, parents, janitors, cafeteria ladies, secretaries, other teachers, the principal, and especially the superintendent. She said the superintendent was an idiot who was the one responsible for the school never having enough books or supplies. She told the students all about it at least once a week in class, especially if she was in a worse mood than normal. The only things she spoke nicely of were her dogs.

Mrs. Austin and her husband raised dogs as a hobby. She talked about them in class and always sort of smiled and called the dogs her babies. Rumor had it that a few years earlier a boy had made Mrs. Austin mad, so she brought one of her dogs to school and it bit off one of his nipples. The other boys and I wanted to know if that rumor was true.

"Go ask her, John," said Stephen.

"No way! You go ask," I replied.

"You two shut up. I'll go ask her," Wade bravely stated.

Stephen and I watched as Wade approached the desk where Mrs. Austin was reading a book. We could see, but not hear what was being said.

"Mrs. Austin?" Wade asked.

"What is it? I'm busy," Mrs. Austin snorted without looking up.

"You raise dogs, don't you?"

Looking up, Mrs. Austin said, "You know I do. Why?"

"Um… did you bring one of your dogs to school a few years ago?"

"Yes. Why?"

Wade stood straight up, his eyes widened, his mouth dropped open and he crossed his arms across his chest, covering his nipples.

"Just wondering," Wade stiffly stated as he backed away from her desk.

Mrs. Austin gave Wade a strange look and then returned to reading her book.

"Well, what did she say?" we asked.

Wade looked back to make sure Mrs. Austin wasn't watching and whispered, "It's true! It's all true!"

"Oh no!" I said. We quickly scattered to our desks and immediately began working on the assignment Mrs. Austin had written on the board.

Class ended and the only thing Stephen, Wade, and I could think about was the nipple-biting dog. We walked down the hall trying to figure out who would get bit first. Herman tagged along behind us bragging about how he had been chosen to play the lead role in Mrs. Smith's class play. We suddenly realized we had forgotten all about the route we had planned to take to gym to avoid Squid.

There he was in the middle of the hall…Squid. Stephen, Wade and I became silent, bunched closely together, looked down and continued walking. Herman continued talking about himself and did not notice.

All of a sudden, "Oh my God! Squid!" screamed Herman. Everyone in the hallway froze and no one made a sound.

Squid stopped, looked to see who had screamed, and began to rock side to side, resembling how a bear stands on its hind legs just before it attacks. At that moment, every boy in the hall except Herman scattered, backs to the wall and staring at Squid.

"No!" Herman screamed as he turned to run. Squid gave chase. As Squid ran past me, he stopped for a moment, looked down and said, "Later." He then took off after Herman.

"What did he mean by that?" Wade frantically asked.

"I don't know! I didn't say a word!" I exclaimed.

"He's gonna kill you!" exclaimed Stephen.

Just then everyone heard Herman scream as he turned to enter a bathroom.

"Is he crazy?" I asked in astonishment. "That's the last place you run if Squid's after you!"

Stephen, Wade and I ran back into Mrs. Austin's room.

"Mrs. Austin! Mrs. Austin!" we all yelled. "Squid's drowning Herman!"

"What are you three talking about?" she demanded to know.

Stephen explained quickly, "Herman's a pain, but nobody deserves to die like that!"

"What?" Mrs. Austin asked in an annoyed voice.

"Okay. Look. Squid chased Herman into the bathroom and he's going to drown him in a toilet!" I clarified. "You've got to save him!"

Slamming her book onto her desk, Mrs. Austin stood up and angrily stomped out of the room and toward the bathroom. All three of us closely followed.

"Back in the room!" she ordered. We turned and ran back into the doorway. We then each peeked back down the hall to watch, overcome with curiosity.

"She's gonna bring the dogs in for sure now," Stephen said. "And we're the ones who made her mad," Wade and I moaned, covering our nipples with our hands and nodding our heads in agreement. "We're all gonna get our nipples bit off." Wade sadly said.

Suddenly Squid ran from the bathroom, saw Mrs. Austin coming, turned and ran the other way. "Get back here!" ordered Mrs. Austin, but Squid was already down the hallway.

"She's too late," Wade said. Stephen and I nodded again in agreement. Just then Herman staggered out of the bathroom, his hair dripping water all over his face and shirt. Herman appeared stunned as he waddled into the hall. His face had no expression, but he was still alive.

"He's alive!" whispered Wade. We looked at each other in amazement.

"Oh, go get some paper towels and dry your head off," Mrs. Austin said coldly. "Then go to the gym and shower off. You'll be fine." As she turned to go back to her room, we quickly ran from the doorway and sat down in our desks in the otherwise unoccupied classroom, and said nothing. As Mrs. Austin entered the room and saw us sitting there, she looked annoyed and barked, "Go to your next class. I'm over this nonsense." We jumped up and hastily headed toward the gym.

"You're next, John," Wade said.

"I didn't do anything!" I protested.

"Doesn't matter to Squid," Stephen observed.

Several weeks passed without incident and I decided I was probably safe. I hoped Squid had forgotten about me.

One Wednesday after lunch, Wade, Stephen and I were returning our lunch trays to the cafeteria after eating in the classroom. There he was…Squid.

"Hey! Hey, you," Squid said as he walked toward us. We stopped. Wade and Stephen took a couple of steps backward. I dropped my tray and backed up against the wall. Squid walked over, looked down at me and asked, "You're an Indian, aren't you?" Then, for reasons I myself did not understand, all fear vanished. I looked up, past Squid's stomach, past his shoulders, and looking Squid directly in the eyes, I said in a confident voice, "I'm Cherokee." I was not going to run. I was standing my ground. I had been bullied enough. I thought of all the strong Cherokee leaders and warriors Grandpa and Dad had told me about, and I was going to be like them. Whatever Squid was going to do, I was ready for it. Stephen and Wade looked at each other in disbelief.

"I moved here from South Dakota," Squid said. "I had lots of Sioux friends there, mostly from the Cheyenne River reservation. My daddy says the Indians get treated really bad and told me we would never do that. Just letting you know I've got your back." Squid gave me a pat on the shoulder, staggering me. Squid then picked up my tray and the paper that had fallen onto the floor. As he handed them to me, he said, "What's your name, kid?"

"John," I said, still in a bit of disbelief. Squid began walking away. Then I called to him, "Hey! What's your name?"

"Kane. Good to know you. All three of you." Then Kane walked away.

I proudly walked on toward the cafeteria with Stephen and Wade following in silent admiration. I had stood my ground and felt great pride.

And everyone still had their nipples.

CHAPTER 15

SNAKES AND BLUEBERRIES

L ate in the summer of 1972 I was visiting my favorite cousin, Logan, who lived on the Boundary, much of which bordered the Great Smoky Mountains National Park.

We were awakened early one morning by Aunt Amy. The sun was beginning to peek over a high ridge and the sky was as blue as the egg of a robin. The morning air was fresh and crisp, filled with the songs of many birds and the occasional distant bark of a dog. A gentle breeze made the leaves on the trees dance and everything seemed to be as it should.

After breakfast, Uncle Matt, Logan and I got into the pick-up truck to go pick blueberries and blackberries high on the ridges near Nantahala, only a short drive from the Boundary.

"Bring back enough for two pies," Aunt Amy called out as the truck began to leave.

"We will!" Logan yelled.

Each of us had a milk carton with the top cut off. We were going to fill them with blueberries. Uncle Matt was planning to fill his with blackberries. After a while we arrived at the picking area. Several cars were already there and some hikers were making their way along a trail. The morning was cooler than usual, but still beautiful. A smooth dirt road with no cars snaked along the ridge. Blueberry and blackberry bushes packed the edges of the road. Picking was going to be easy. Uncle Matt headed off toward a stand of blackberry bushes.

"You boys stay together and stay on the road," Uncle Matt said as he wandered away.

"We will," we replied in unison.

A few elderly women from the Boundary were carefully picking berries. They wore aprons and wore bandanas covering their heads in the old way. The ladies worked quietly. The boys noticed they were carefully picking one or two berries at a time, leaving most on the bushes. Logan and I also knew the elderly were to always get first choice, so we waited until the ladies had moved on to a different bush before we attempted picking. After about ten minutes Logan and I noticed that although the elderly women were picking slower than we were, the ladies had far more berries.

"Maybe we're eating too many," Logan observed.

"I think you're right. We better quit eating or we'll never get enough for two pies," I said.

We made our way down the road. The sun was up now and the day was getting a bit warmer.

"Think Uncle Matt will let us cool off in the river on the way back?" I asked.

"Sure he will. Always does," Logan assured me.

We almost had enough berries for two pies.

"John, do you remember the Cherokee word for rattlesnake?" asked Logan quietly.

After thinking for a moment I said, "U-tsa-na-ti."

"Well there's an U-tsa-na-ti between your feet," Logan very stiffly stated.

"Yeah, right," I said as I looked down.

"AHHHHHH!" I screamed. I stumbled backwards trying to get away from the rattler. My feet slid out from under me, my box of blueberries sailed high into the air. I landed on my butt in the middle of the road, dust flew everywhere and my blueberries rained down upon one of the elderly ladies. She turned around, calmly looked at me sitting frozen in the middle of the road. She then turned to Logan, calmly said something to him in Cherokee and they both laughed. The lady returned to picking berries.

"What's so funny?" I demanded. I wished I could speak the language fluently, but knew that would never be. Dad had told me it was for my own good, and I trusted him.

"She said the rattlesnake is asleep. It's just warming itself on the rock and was not going to bite you," Logan smiled.

"How was I supposed to know?" I asked as Logan helped me back to my feet. I picked up my carton which was now almost void of blueberries.

"We better pick fast," Logan observed.

"Yeah," I agreed.

As we were finishing refilling my carton, Uncle Matt reappeared.

"You boys ready?" he asked.

The three of us walked back to the truck. Uncle Matt noticed I was covered in dust, but said nothing about it. On the way down the mountain Logan shared the story of the rattlesnake with his dad. Even I had to laugh at it now.

Uncle Matt pulled the truck into a campground next to the Oconaluftee River, which flows right through Cherokee, the main town on the Boundary.

"You two go cool off. I'll be in there," he stated as he gestured to a small campground store.

We kicked off our shoes and socks and took our shirts off. We walked down a path toward the river looking for a good place to enter. We stopped for a few seconds and about that time I felt something smooth sliding across the top of my feet. Two slim snakes with intricate coloring slid across my feet, not seeming to even notice them, and continuing toward the water. "At least they weren't rattlesnakes," I said.

Logan stood still for a moment, shook his head and asked, "Do you remember what wo-di-ge a sko-li means?"

I thought for a minute, but replied, "No. Why?"

"It means copperhead, John. Those were copperheads that just crawled across your feet."

I quickly turned to see where the snakes had gone but they were out of sight.

"A rattlesnake and two copperheads in one day and I didn't get bit. Cool!" I proudly said.

"Lucky," Logan replied.

We scampered into the river. Logan walked in and sat in a pool of water between large, smooth boulders. I walked in as far as letting water reach just above my knees.

"Get in!" Logan called to me. But, still not used to the coldness of the water, I stood still. Logan stood up, cupped his hands, dipped them carefully into the water and thrust the cold, cold water right between my legs. "There. Now get in!" Logan laughed.

I bent over, unable to breathe or speak, wanting to pick up a boulder and smash Logan flat, but the anger left and instead I whipped an armful of water right into Logan's face. Logan continued to laugh. The water fight was on and we no longer felt the coldness of the water and wildly splashed and threw water at each other, oblivious to the rest of the world. A f t e r several minutes of splashing, we both sat down in a new spot, as we had stirred up sediment during the splashing, and we didn't want to sit in it. We relaxed and caught our breath and neither of us had a worry in the world. "Water is healing," Logan said.

"Sure is," I agreed. As I sat in the flowing waters of the Oconaluftee, the dust and dirt which had caked onto me when I fell picking blueberries slowly dissolved and floated as underwater clouds away from me, as did every worry in my world.

Later that afternoon as we pulled into the driveway at Logan's house, I couldn't wait to tell Aunt Amy all about the great snake and water adventures.

CHAPTER 16

THE FIRE

It was a beautiful September day and I had just begun seventh grade. The bullies had all gone on to high school and I was once again enjoying school. Dad was at work, but mom had relapsed and was still asleep. Dad was at lunch when he decided to take a boxed lunch home to mom. Dad noticed that every traffic light he encountered on the way home was green, something that just does not happen in Knoxville.

Dad arrived home and as he entered the house, he smelled the faint odor of smoke. He thought perhaps mom had burned some toast. He put Mom's lunch on the kitchen counter and walked upstairs where the bedrooms were located. The smell of smoke became pronounced and Dad rushed to open the bedroom door. As he did, a blast of extremely hot air thrust him backward against the opposite wall of the hallway almost knocking him out. At that moment of partial consciousness, Dad's military training kicked in. He crawled across the floor, around the foot of the bed to where Mom was unconscious, pulled her onto his back and began crawling military style back out of the room. As he rounded the bed, the floor beneath him began to sag. When he reached the hallway, he flung mom over his shoulders and ran down the stairs and out onto the front lawn. At that very moment the windows of the house began exploding from the heat and the air conditioner in my bedroom window crashed to the ground. Dad passed out.

That day some workers were laying sewer lines through our back yard. Droopy, Garfunkel and their nine new puppies were boarding at the veterinarian's to keep them from running away, as the fence around the back yard had to be removed for the sewer lines to be laid. The workers saw what was happening, took Dad's car keys from him and moved the Rambler out of harm's way. They also called for ambulances. A couple of workers stayed with Dad and Mom while others smashed out a large pane glass window downstairs and carried out as much furniture as possible before things became too dangerous. The ambulances arrived and took my parents to the hospital. Dad was treated and released, but Mom was admitted to the Intensive Care Unit (ICU) with smoke inhalation. The prognosis was very grim.

Meanwhile at school, the principal, a very tall, nice man, asked my teacher to step into the hall. He spoke to her for a few moments and everyone in the class saw her gasp and place her hand over her mouth. She reentered the classroom and sat at her desk, saying nothing and looking quite pale. A few minutes later the office called for me to check out. Confused but happy to leave early, I took my book bag out of my locker along with the basketball I had taken to school. When I arrived in the office the school secretary asked, "Do you know this woman?" Puzzled, I said, "Yes. It's Mrs. McGill, our neighbor." Mrs. McGill softly stated, "John, there was a fire at your house, and the hospital is taking good care of your parents. I'm going to take you to my house for right now." My mouth dropped open and I was in shock. I followed Mrs. McGill to her car but said nothing all the way to her house, which was about two hundred yards from our house.

When we arrived at the McGill's house, I - book bag and basketball in hand - slowly ascended the small hill between our houses. I could see the heat rising before I could see what was left of the house. The last of the carport was burning and only the brick chimney stood. All else was smoldering ruins and ashes. I stood in disbelief. Mark Noble's mother came over to comfort me, but I hardly noticed. A large crowd had gathered to watch the spectacle, but I knew none of them.

About that time the minister, Dr. Jackson, a wonderful man whose kind voice and warm smile always put me at ease, arrived on the scene and found me. "John, your parents are being checked out at the hospital. I have arranged for you to spend the next two nights with the Ford family," he reassuringly told me.

That night I cried myself to sleep, feeling an emptiness so overwhelming it physically hurt. The next day at school when I entered the classroom wearing the same clothes as the day before, all the students stopped and stared at me, not making a sound. I was embarrassed but said nothing. Mark Noble finally came over to me and said, "I hope your mom survives." I asked what he meant. Then Mark, realizing I had not been told, said, "John, I'm sorry. So sorry! I thought you knew." I replied in a shaking voice, "Nobody told me! I want to go to the hospital now!" I was stuck at school, as no one was available to take me to the hospital to see my Mom. A teacher told me I could not visit the ICU because I was only twelve years old. I accomplished nothing academically that day as all I could think about was the probability I would never see my mom again.

I stayed with the Fords for two nights then would spend one night each in a variety of homes within the school district. Finally, the Noble family told me I could stay with them for several weeks. I did not see my parents for more than a week until at last word came that my mother was out of ICU and I could visit. Dad picked me up and drove to the hospital. I slowly entered the room where Mom was, not knowing what to expect. She saw me and smiled as if she had won a million dollars. I was so relieved I took two deep breaths, ran around the bed and gave Mom a hug.

"How long will it take to rebuild the house?" I anxiously asked.

"John, we can't rebuild. The house was under insured by twenty-five thousand dollars," Dad sadly stated.

"But where will we go? What will we do?" I desperately asked.

"Your mother and I will stay in a motel. You will stay with the Nobles and others until something can be worked out, and I don't know how long that will be," Dad replied.

"What about Droopy and Garfunkel? What about the puppies?" I implored.

"They're safe at the vet's. You will see them soon." Mom said.

I was dirty, I smelled from not bathing, and I looked extremely ragged. I was unaware of how badly I smelled, but the other children at school understood what I was going through and were very kind to me.

The end of September came and I still had not seen my beloved dogs. Dad had searched among his friends for someone who would take care of the dogs until we could find another house. A friend agreed to take care of Droopy, Garfunkel, and all nine puppies. In exchange, Dad told his friend he could keep the pick of the litter. He then phoned me, at the Noble's to tell me about the dogs and promised to take me to see them the weekend after next. I was elated and began to count the days.

Three days prior to my scheduled visit with Droopy and Garfunkel, Mrs. Noble called me to the phone and somberly said, "Your dad needs to speak to you."

"Hello? Dad?" I answered.

"John, I hate to tell you this, but someone stole Droopy, Garfunkel, and all nine puppies," Dad said.

"Who?" I screamed in a panic. "Did you call the police? When did it happen?"

In a very sad voice Dad informed me the dogs were gone, nothing could be done to get them back and that we would never see them again.

When I hung up the phone, I silently walked out the back door of the Nobles' house, got on my bike and rode to the ruins of my home. The dog house was still intact and the faint smell of the dogs was still present. As the sun began to go down, I fell to my knees at the dog house door, still in disbelief anyone would steal my beloved Droopy, Garfunkel, and all nine puppies. As realization sat in, I slumped to a sitting position and leaned against the dog house, and as the sun moved lower in the western sky, tears silently flowed down my face as I shook in gut-wrenching agony. When total darkness engulfed the earth, my soul screamed to the heavens, but the heavens did not respond.

Mid-November rolled around and I was still homeless, staying with a variety of families for one night at a time, but mostly with the Nobles, who would keep me for a week at a time.

After arriving at the Nobles' after school one day, Mrs. Noble told Mark and me to get in the car. She drove us to another neighborhood a few miles away and pointed to a house. "John, there is your new house. Your parents closed on it today. You move in tomorrow." Mrs. Noble excitedly told me. I was ecstatic.

The following day my parents moved in to the house with what little furniture they had. The bed in my room was borrowed, as was the dresser, but the small desk was one that had been saved by the men laying the sewer lines the day of the fire. I had very few material goods, but I felt great.

Mom entered my room and sat down. "Sweetheart, I know we did not see you for three months and for that I am so sorry, but I want you to know why. You know I had started taking medicine again. I was in rehab for the past three months and I am clean and rid of all medicines. I am so sorry I put you through that and I have good news. I am going back to college to earn my teaching degree and I will become a teacher so we will have more money. John, your nightmare is over." She then leaned over and hugged me for the first time since I could remember.

CHAPTER 17

CHERRY BELLIES

I was still bothered by the fact I was short - about 4' 9" tall, weighed about 91 pounds, and that my voice had not even begun to change. Most all of my friends were much taller and had deep voices. But my one bright spot was that I still ran faster than any of them. Another good thing about seventh grade was everyone went to classes with other students who were making the same grades. That meant the Pea Creek rednecks were all together and I had none of them in any of my classes.

A new kid had moved to town. His name was Javier Texador, but everybody called him Javi. He was from Puerto Rico, and he and I became good friends. Javi was slightly taller than me with brown skin and eyes and black wavy hair. He liked to laugh and always seemed to have a smile on his face. He was a thin kid, but a fast runner and a good ball player. Javi and I seemed to have a lot in common and we were very comfortable around each other.

About the same time Javi had moved in, the big mean eighth graders had started giving other kids cherry bellies. Cherry bellies usually happened in bathrooms, locker rooms or during recess when teachers stopped paying attention. At least three or four boys would grab the victim's arms and legs and raise him up. Another kid would pull up the victim's shirt and then others would repeatedly slap the victim's stomach until it became red, thus the name cherry belly. Everybody knew they would get it one day, but, being small, I avoided eighth graders as much as possible. Like all the other boys, I gave my friends cherry bellies. I was careful not to slap too hard, because I was small, hoped that when it came my turn, they might go easy on me.

On the playground one March afternoon, a group of boys grabbed Javi and began giving him a cherry belly. I would not slap Javi. In fact, after seeing it go for a little bit, in as deep of a voice as I could speak said, "That should do it." The others thought someone else had said it and they let him go. After they left, I said, "I didn't slap you. I was the one who said to stop."

"Thanks," Javi said. "But your turn is coming soon. I won't slap you either."

About a week later during a class change, I walked into the restroom and immediately realized my turn had come. I didn't fight it. Legs were grabbed, arms grabbed, shirt pulled up and the slapping began.

"He's not turning very red," one boy said.

"He's brown. I guess they don't turn red like normal people," said another.

"Okay. That's enough. We can let him go now," said a boy. They let me down and I walked out of the restroom as fast as I could, because just about that time one of the boys said, "Who said to let him go? That was too fast…. John!!" But it was too late. The unwritten cherry belly rule was you could only get cherry bellied once a year and I had gotten mine. With my stomach barely stinging, I felt proud, as I had outsmarted all the other boys in the bathroom and had gotten off far easier than anyone else.

CHAPTER 18

THE BAMBOO PADDLE

The social studies teacher, Mr. Blake, was a big man with a large belly and nobody messed with him. He had slicked-back black hair and he always wore solid-colored shirts. Rumor had it he had a varnished bamboo paddle with holes in it in his closet and once he would use it on someone, they would limp forever. Mark Noble, the smartest kid in class swore he had seen it, so everybody knew it had to be true. Almost everybody liked Mr. Blake, even though he enjoyed paddling students. He was a good teacher who said funny things and if one of the Pea Creek rednecks started after anyone, all they had to do was call for Mr. Blake and they would be safe.

Mr. Blake arranged the desks into groups of four. Javi, Mark and the biggest boy in the class, Ethan, and I sat together. One day shortly before spring break, everyone was supposed to be working on a group project. My group was not doing much work, so Mr. Blake walked up and demanded to see our work. When we could not produce any, Mr. Blake said, "Just what

I thought. The only thing I've seen moving over here today are elbows and buttholes. Get to work."

"Yes sir," we said in unison, trying hard not to laugh.

Mr. Blake turned to the class and told everyone he was stepping out for a minute and he expected everyone to be working and to keep the noise to a minimum. After Mr. Blake had been gone a few minutes, Ethan, the goofiest kid in the group started singing like an opera lady. Mark and I thought it was funny and joined in. After a few seconds, all three of us were standing and giving a concert to the class. Javi did not join in and was trying to get us to stop, waving his

hands back and forth, shaking his head side to side and mouthing "no."

Sudden silence. Instant fear. Mr. Blake was standing in the classroom door and he was not happy. His face was like stone, his eyes were aflame, fists clenched so tight his knuckles were white, and he had a slight snarl on his mouth.

"Come here, boys," Mr. Blake growled in a slow, almost whispering, yet terrifying voice. Mark, Ethan and I knew we were doomed. Mr. Blake calmly marched us into the hall and asked, "What were you three doing?"

"Singing, sir," Mark said as he looked at the floor.

"And you Ethan?"

"Same thing, sir."

"Same with you John?" he asked.

"Yes sir. A little bit."

"Any at all, John?"

"Yes sir."

"Guilty. Wait here." Mr. Blake slowly walked back into the room. The three of us could hear the closet door open and close. As Mr. Blake came back into the hall, we all knew life as we had known it was over. There it was in Mr. Blake's huge right hand, just as Mark had said. Varnished. Bamboo. Four rows of holes drilled through it.

"*Our butts are gonna look like dice,*" I thought.

"Who wants to go first, gentlemen?" Mr. Blake asked in a quiet, emotionless voice.

Nobody moved. All three of us looked at each other then the floor.

"Get over here, Ethan." Ethan walked over. "Bend over and grab your ankles." Mr. Blake grabbed Ethan by the back of his belt, lifted him onto his toes with this left hand, and pulled back the bamboo destroyer...

WHAM!! WHAM!! It echoed down the empty hallway and back. I was scared to death. Ethan and Mark had had their growth spurts. I was still little and knowing I would be the one scarred for life. I began to tremble.

Then, a ray of hope. On the second impact on Ethan's butt, the paddle broke in half. I looked up at Mark with a slight look of relief. "Don't move, boys," stated Mr. Blake. "I have a spare." Walking a little faster, Mr. Blake re-entered the classroom. The closet door opened. A few seconds later it slammed shut. I was terrified. I stared straight ahead but really was not looking at anything. My mouth was dry, palms sweaty and my trembling became worse. Mark stared straight ahead. Mr. Blake re-emerged with a piece of a sawed off two-by-four, about eighteen inches long.

"Mark. Grab your ankles." Same thing. Lifted up, slammed twice. I was hoping the two-by-four would break, but it didn't.

"Your turn, John. Bend over and grab your ankles." fart

"*The farther over I bend, the tighter my butt muscles will be and worse I'll get hurt.*" I thought. As I began bending over, I looked up at my executioner out of the corner of his eye and sheepishly said, "I'm not very flexible and I'm little..."

"Grab 'em now!" WHAM!!! WHAM!!! Echoes followed. I stood up and took a step. My butt was stinging, but I could walk. Taking a deep breath of relief, the three of us limped back into the class. No one was talking. No one was working. Everybody's eyes were fixed on the three of us. We had survived.

I never mentioned the paddling at home, because I knew if Mom or Dad found out, I would be severely punished. The three of us agreed to never speak of the paddling, especially in front of any adults.

Our opera days had come to a very painful end.

CHAPTER 19

THE SUMMER
OF 1973

Seventh grade had ended. I was still short and my voice showed no signs of changing. I thought it never would. My favorite cousin, Logan, lived on the Boundary and I loved spending time with him. We were the same age and like me, Logan was still small and had a high voice. Another thing I liked about the Boundary was I fit in; I looked like so many others. Nobody ever made a big deal out of being Indian. I did not like the fact so many people on the Boundary lived in poverty. That bothered me. Some stores stayed open all year, but many did not. Many families found it very difficult to make it through the isolated winters. Even though much of the Boundary bordered the Great Smoky Mountains National Park, it seemed the tourists preferred Gatlinburg on the Tennessee side, especially in the winter. The county most of the Boundary was in was one of the poorest in North Carolina.

Knoxville was the city most visitors used to get to the Great Smoky Mountains National Park, and they usually spent their time and money in Gatlinburg. Cherokee was more isolated than Gatlinburg. The seasonal jobs on the Boundary would last from late spring until the leaves finished changing colors in the fall, and then unemployment would skyrocket. People wanted to work. The people were not lazy. It was just that good-paying, permanent jobs were few and far between on the Boundary.

On Monday, July 9, 1973, Mom, Dad, and I loaded up the Rambler and set off for Logan's house.

I was going to stay for two weeks this time and was excited. Mom and dad stayed one night, then drove back home after lunch the following day. "See you in a couple of weeks, John," Dad said.

"Be good," Mom said. As my parents drove off, Logan and I ran to Logan's room to see what we could do. An afternoon thunderstorm rolled in, so we sat around and talked.

"You're lucky you live here," I said to Logan.

"Why? You have it better in Knoxville."

"Nobody here makes fun of you. Well, except for those stupid girls you told me about. And nobody tells you about their Indian princess granny."

"But you never go hungry or freeze in the winter. Remember the soup we had at lunch?"

"Yeah. What about it?"

"The meat. Did you like it?"

"Well, yes. Why?"

"You know where my dad got it?"

"At the grocery store."

"No, John. He took an old blowgun and shot a bird out of a tree. We have to get a lot of our food from the woods. All you do is get in a car and drive to a grocery store."

"I didn't know," I said. "My mom grows a lot of our vegetables and cans them for the winter, too."

"I'll bet she does that 'cause she wants to, not 'cause she has to."

"I don't know. Never asked."

"I've been to your house in the winter. Y'uns got electric heat. We gotta go chop wood in the fall and hope it lasts all winter. Ever go out in the winter and dig up yellowjacket grubs?

No. Why would I do that?" I asked with a puzzled look on my face.

"I do every winter. Mom boils them and adds some stuff and we eat them. They taste pretty good," Logan remarked.

"Yuck. I had no idea stuff like that went on." I replied sadly.

"Well it does. All the time. You've got it way easier over there."

"Guess you're right. But in a way you have it easier over here. Do people make fun of you and do things to you 'cause you're Indian? No. That's hard to put up with. And most everybody else has way more money than us. You ought to see the cars they drive and the stuff they wear. They're rich and they make fun of me 'cause we're not."

"I guess we both have our own problems, John. But at least yours can't kill you."

"Yeah. You're right. But I still like staying here," I said as I hit Logan in the face with a pillow. And a wonderful, laughter-filled pillow fight for the ages ensued.

The days passed quickly. A couple of days we swam in the river. The water was always cold and I still had a hard time getting used to it. All the local kids jumped right in. Two very pale large girls splashed water on me.

"You're not from around here are you?" they laughed.

"No. I'm here visiting Logan."

"You're afraid of the water!" the girls laughingly taunted.

"I am not. I'm just not used to the temperature."

"Leave us alone," Logan told them. "Go bother somebody else."

The girls whispered something to each other, laughed, rolled their eyes and walked away.

"What's their problem?" I asked Logan.

"Who knows?" replied Logan. "They're mean to everybody. Dad says it's because they don't like themselves. I think it's because they were just born mean."

The following Tuesday, July 17th, Logan and I decided to go to town and run around. We asked Uncle Matt for a ride to town. Uncle Matt drove an old Ford pickup truck. He always said Ford made the best pickups. "Every other brand of pickup rusts out too fast. Always get a Ford," he would say. The truck was brown with quite a few dents, but no rust. Uncle Matt had told me it had "240 air conditioning," but I did not see an air conditioner.

Uncle Matt explained that 240 air conditioning was when he rolled down both windows and drove 40 miles an hour. The tires were worn, but no threads were showing. Three of the hubcaps were gone. Uncle Matt said he liked the truck because it never broke down. Unlike the Rambler, the radio worked and it would go even in hard rain. Logan and I piled into the back of the truck while Uncle Matt and Aunt Amy rode in the cabin.

"You two stay seated, you hear me? Don't want you falling out," Aunt Amy ordered.

"Okay, mom," said Logan.

"Okay," I stated.

The ride to town only took about fifteen minutes but it seemed to me it had a few million hard bumps. Logan didn't seem to notice them.

"Meet us right back here at 4:00," Uncle Matt instructed as he dropped us off next to the new museum that was under construction.

"Okay. I got on a watch," Logan said.

We spent the next couple of hours playing on the trail that led up to the outdoor theater, where the seasonal play about the Eastern Cherokee history was held. We also spent time tossing rocks into the river at the bottom of the hill.

We were walking down a sidewalk when a bus load of tourists was walking in our direction. "Look, Ralph," said one woman, "Indians!"

"That one looks kind of Chinese," the man replied.

"They're not dressed like Indians," another man said.

"Let's get out of here," Logan whispered to me. We turned around and ran to the corner. I wanted to cross the road but Logan wanted to turn right and get away from the rude woman. So we ran down the street past the fair grounds, which were just behind the new museum being built, and then stopped. About that time I spotted an old tennis ball on the side of the road. Logan and I tossed, kicked and bounced the ball back and forth for a while. When that got old, we decided to just run around some more, tossing the ball as we went. Logan had the ball and turned right, crossing in front of the small building that housed the Enrollment Office. Dad had said he felt sorry for the people who worked there, because they had to deal with a lot of people who wanted to enroll, or become official members of the tribe, but were not eligible. Dad said he would not like that job; too many people getting mad at you and all.

Logan threw the ball, but it was flying over my head. I decided he would make a phenomenal catch and impress anyone who might be watching. As I began to jump, my foot slipped on some loose gravel and down I went on my right knee. Hard.

"You alright?" Logan yelled, as he trotted over to me. I was sitting up in a cloud of dirt and dust.

I felt an unusual pain in my leg. I bent forward and looked down. Blood was pouring from my right knee. I was in pain, but only noticed the split knee. I didn't even notice the smaller abrasions and cuts.

"That's bad!" Logan yelled as he took off his t-shirt and put it over the gash. Give me your t-shirt, he ordered. I gave it to him and he tied it around the injured knee.

"Stay here. I'll get some help," he ordered.

"Where would I go?" I yelled back as I grabbed a handful of dirt and small gravel and threw it in Logan's direction.

A couple of minutes later, which seemed like forever to me, a nice lady emerged from the Enrollment Office with Logan.

"It's pretty bad so I bandaged it. Got to stop the bleeding," Logan told the lady.

"You need to go to the hospital," the lady told us. "Do your parents have a phone where I can reach them?"

Logan told her I was his cousin visiting from out of town and that his parents were in town somewhere but would not be back for more than another hour. The nice lady, whose name turned out to be Mrs. King, put us in her car and drove us up the hill to the IHS (Indian Health Service) hospital. She and Logan helped me inside and sat me down. She briefly spoke to an attendant and returned to us. By this time, the dull pain had turned to throbbing pain that at times ached as bad as a toothache.

"What kind of car are they driving?" she asked.

"A brown Ford pick-up," Logan replied.

"Do you know where they may be right now?"

"In town somewhere. They're supposed to meet us at the new museum at 4:00."

"Okay, dear. Thank you," she said as she left.

About ten people sat in the waiting room and almost no one was talking. Grey metal chairs lined the walls and formed a row in the center of the room. The tile floors needed to be waxed and the windows were small, letting in little sunlight. From the outside, the hospital was built with a lot of stone and looked pleasant, but inside it was somewhat foreboding to me. I recalled Grandpa telling me to avoid hospitals. "People go to hospitals to die," Grandpa had often said. I heard sounds of people walking around and the air had a slight smell of rubbing alcohol.

By this time I was sweating and felt as if I was going to throw up. An elderly woman in the waiting room noticed. She took an old blue bandana from her head, ran some water onto it, folded it and handed it to Logan. She said something to him in Cherokee, but I could not understand. I didn't need to, for I could tell she was kind and caring. Logan quietly replied in Cherokee and placed the bandana over my forehead. It felt good and it helped to keep me from vomiting.

After what seemed to be years, a worker came over. Logan quietly spoke with her. I did not listen to what was said. All I could think about was how horrible the pain in my knee was, now radiating throughout my leg.

The worker walked back to the counter, looked through all sorts of files and returned. "What did you say his name was?"

Logan repeated the information.

"His parents' names? Perhaps an address?"

Logan wrote it down. The worker went back to the desk. I was starting to get upset. "What's taking so long, Logan?"

The worker returned and stated, "Our records don't show he's enrolled."

"So what?!" Logan pleaded. "He's my cousin! He's Cherokee and he's hurt bad!"

"I'm sorry. We can only treat enrolled Indians. It's the law," stated the worker in an apologetic voice. "You'll have to take him to the hospital in Bryson City. Besides, the injury is not life-threatening."

In the meantime, Mrs. King had located Logan's parents. Uncle Matt rushed in to the waiting room and asked what had happened. Logan told him the entire story. Uncle Matt and Logan helped me up, but by then I could not walk. My leg was in too much pain and I was dizzy.

The two pale girls I had met at the river were badly sunburned and sat in the waiting room with their shoulders and faces partially smeared with some type of white cream.

"Greetings," one of them said sarcastically.

"Not enrolled!" the other one sneered as I was carried by.

"Shut up! He's way more Indian than either of you!" Logan yelled at them.

"Come on Logan. Ignore them," Uncle Matt ordered.

I was carefully placed in the cabin of the truck. The bleeding had mostly stopped, but not the pain. Dried blood was all over my leg. Aunt Amy held me and tried to comfort me.

Angry and struggling to speak, I asked, "What were those white people doing in there? They get helped and I don't?!"

In an apologetic voice Uncle Matt said, "They're enrolled. You're not."

"But they're white," I protested.

"Not in the eyes of the BIA," Logan said in disgust.

Uncle Matt and Aunt Amy took me to the hospital in Bryson City, which was a town only a few miles off the Boundary. Things were slow there as well. The hospital called long distance to get my Dad's insurance information and permission before finally treating me. It was extremely painful as they removed small rocks and other debris from the swollen knee. The nurses would slowly lift the top part of the gash to expose any debris, and when they did, I felt as if my leg would explode. I laid back and placed my hands over my forehead and bowed my back up trying not to scream. Whatever the liquid the doctors were squirting into the wound stung badly. I was breathing hard and deep, but I kept from screaming. They finally had it cleaned out and stitched it up. Fourteen stitches. The doctor wrapped my knee, told me not to bend it or get it wet for several days, and then gave me a set of crutches to use.

Back at Logan's house I said, "Most of the people at the hospital were Cherokees, but I know I saw some white people in there. And, they were getting treated. Even those mean girls. Are they Indians?"

"Yes," replied Aunt Amy. "You can't judge based on looks. Their families were on the 1924 Baker Roll. John, I'm afraid your family wasn't."

"I know the story," I said as I looked down at my knee. "My great-grandfather got into trouble with the law and ran off. He got drunk and beat a wealthy white man almost to death."

"Yes, sweetheart, he did. And, he went to Indian Territory but left there and ended up in Tennessee."

"I know that too," I said. "And he was an alcoholic. So was my grandfather."

Gently, Aunt Amy said, "Your great-grandmother, Lilly, died in childbirth and your great-grandfather, Jesse, turned to the bottle and never recovered. Both Jesse and your grandfather were alcoholics and never showed up to get on the 1924 roll."

"So, because of them I'm not enrolled," I said through clenched teeth. "That's so unfair! I'm more Indian than a lot of those people at the hospital today! This is stupid!"

"Calm down, John," Uncle Matt said. "You've been through enough today. Yes, it's unfair. But don't blame the tribe."

"Blame the stupid wannabees!" Logan angrily blurted out. "Dad, you've even said it. If it wasn't for wannabees, John could probably get enrolled."

"Enough, Logan," Uncle Matt said. "Yes, I've said that." Shaking his head, Uncle Matt explained. "Look, boys, we all know it's almost impossible to run into a white man in the south who doesn't think he's part Cherokee, right?"

"Princesses," I said with disgust in my voice.

"Exactly," said Uncle Matt. "The tribe has no choice but to stick with the 1924 roll. Otherwise, every white man in the south would be over here enrolling and before you know it, the tribe would be destroyed. John, as hard as it is to say, you're one of the orphans."

Although I hated to hear those words, I understood.

With my voice shaking, my knee throbbing, and eyes tearing up, I said, "At home I'm 'that Indian kid.' Over here I'm not even enrolled and they treat me like I'm a white kid." I could not speak any more, as I felt completely despondent.

Logan held my arm. "Look, John, you're my cousin. And you are Cherokee, no matter what anybody says."

"The sins of the father, John. The sins of the father," Aunt Amy sadly whispered.

CHAPTER 20

BACK OVER THE MOUNTAINS

A unt Amy had telephoned Mom and Dad after returning from the hospital. Dad wanted to leave immediately to get me, but the Rambler had broken down again and it would be two or three days before it would be repaired.

The next couple of days dragged by as I was on crutches and could not move well. Uncle Matt took us for a drive on the Blue Ridge Parkway, but Logan and I really wanted to just hang around together.

Mom and Dad arrived a few days later. They stayed overnight at Uncle Matt's. Logan and I were sad because we knew we would not see each other again for several months.

The next morning Dad and Logan loaded up the Rambler. It was lightly raining and I wondered if the car would start. It did. Dad drove into town and stopped at the Enrollment Office. I knew we needed to thank Mrs. King for her kindness. Mom chose to stay in the car. Dad took out a folder and he and I slowly entered the building. Mrs. King saw me and she got up, walked over and hugged me.

"How are you doing, honey?" she asked.

"I'm okay. Just a little sore. Thank you for helping me the other day."

Dad introduced himself and thanked Mrs. King as well. Then, to my surprise, Dad asked to see William Lively, the Enrollment Officer. Mrs. King checked to see if he was free.

"He'll see you in just a few minutes, as soon as he gets off the phone," Mrs. King told Dad.

"That's fine," he answered.

After about five minutes, Mr. Lively came out of his office and introduced himself to Dad. The two men went into the office and closed the door. I sat near Mrs. King's desk thumbing through old magazines that were of no interest to me. After about ten minutes, Dad and Mr. Lively emerged from the office, still talking.

"...and so the older rolls won't do," I overheard Dad say.

"Jim, I wish I could tell you otherwise, but the BIA wouldn't stand for it. I must follow the rules," stated Mr. Lively.

"I completely understand your position," Dad said. The two men shook hands and then Dad turned to me and told me they were finished and to go to the car.

"Will I see you next time you're here?" Mrs. King asked me as she gave a warm smile.

"I promise," I said.

I knew my dad had tried to enroll, but could not because his family had missed the 1924 roll. I felt down and hardly spoke a word as we drove through the rain over the Smoky Mountains. The temperature was cold and clouds clung low to the mountains. Rain was steady and fog engulfed the car. As far as I was concerned, fog had engulfed my entire world.

I felt despondent. "*Please God,*" I thought. "*Please make something good happen. I'm so tired of all this bad luck.*"

The skies began to clear as the Rambler made its way into Knoxville and by the time we arrived home the sun was shining. Dad began unloading the car with Mom's help.

"Can I help?" I asked.

"No, John. You stay off your feet," Mom replied.

"Well, I'll help …" I could not believe my ears. I spoke again. "If I can help …"

"*It really happened!*" I thought. My voice had just cracked. Not once, but twice! "*My voice is changing,*" I thought with great joy.

I yelled, "Yes!" as I fell backwards onto the wet grass.

"Are you alright?" Dad asked as he and Mom looked at each other with puzzled looks on their faces.

"I'm great!!" I exclaimed as my voice cracked again. "Everything is going to be great!!" I knew I would soon grow and I was elated.

CHAPTER 21

NEVER THE ANSWER

I entered high school at 5' 10" and 130 pounds. In tenth grade I transferred to Bearden High School. I wanted to run track for the legendary track coach, Bob LeSueur. The main downside to transferring was leaving behind the friends I had known since elementary school.

I arrived home after cross-country practice one October afternoon to find both my parents waiting for me at the front door. Mom and Dad both looked very serious and quiet and told me to have a seat in the living room. I had never seen my parents like that and knew something was wrong. I walked to the living room and sat on the couch, wondering what was happening.

"We have some sad news about one of your friends," said Mom.

"What's going on?" I inquired.

Mom and Dad looked at one another for a moment, then Dad quietly stated, "Mark Noble committed suicide last night."

"No way!" I protested. "I saw him at the convenient store two days ago and he was laughing and joking with people. You must be wrong."

"His body is at the mortuary," Dad insisted.

For me, the shock and disbelief were overwhelming and time seemed to stop. "He's only fifteen. How? Why?" I demanded.

"No one knows," Mom said in a sad voice. "We're so sorry."

"Alright!" I shouted as I stormed off to my room. I shut the door and sat stunned for what seemed like forever.

The following several days were a blur, and then came the day of visitation. When my parents and I arrived at the mortuary, I was still hoping a huge mistake had happened and that somehow Mark was still alive. But when I saw Mark lying lifeless in the grey metal casket, I knew it was all too real. I could only stare and wonder why Mark would have killed himself. After several minutes of trying to process everything, I saw Mark's parents sitting nearby. I walked over to them and before I could say a word, Mr. Noble said, "We want you to be one of the pallbearers, John. You were always such a good friend to Mark." I agreed and the rest of the visit became a blur.

The following morning was the funeral. Five of Mark's other friends and I carried the very heavy casket from the hearse to the grave site. A minister talked, but I heard nothing he said. I could only run memories I had with Mark through my head. When the minister finished, I once again reentered the sad moment. Mark's dad walked over and hugged me and the other pallbearers. Even though it was a beautiful day everything seemed surreal.

I happened to look up the hill and saw my Dad. A single tear was rolling down his face. I had never seen Dad cry. He drove me home, a ride that seemed to take forever. When we arrived home, I went to my room and listened to music for a while. I then came out of my room and said to Dad, "I know Mark isn't hurting any more but now the rest of us are."

"You're right, John," Dad sadly replied. "Suicide is never the answer. Never."

CHAPTER 22

1976

June of 1976 rolled around and some of my friends could drive. One of my good friends, Chris Stevens, attended the same church, played on the same recreation league basketball team and was encouraging me to try out for the school's Junior Varsity basketball team in the fall.

"With the way you can jump, you'll make the team easy," Chris told me.

"Thanks, but my other basketball skills aren't as good as yours. I really want to run for Coach LeSueur. I just wanted to run track but he's making me run cross-country to get in shape for track." I replied. "But I'll come watch you play some."

"Okay. Sounds good." agreed Chris.

It was a Saturday night and Chris had worked overtime at his part-time job, leaving about 1:00 in the morning. He was very sleepy as he began his drive home, which was about six miles from work. Chris buckled his seatbelt and started the car. As he drove west on Kingston Pike he began to nod off, only to shake his head to awaken and clear his head. Staying awake became more difficult with every mile, but he knew he could make it home. He began to doze off again.

Sunday morning I walked in to a room full of sad-looking youth at church.

"What's going on?" I asked.

"You don't know?" asked one of the Sunday School teachers.

"Know what?" I inquired with a concerned voice.

"Chris Stevens was in a serious car accident last night. He's at the University of Tennessee Medical Center," the teacher stated. "He apparently fell asleep on the way home from work last night and hit a telephone pole."

"But he drives his mom's Mercedes. Those are super safe!" I argued.

"It's an old Mercedes with only a lap belt. He hit his head against the steering wheel extremely hard suffered brain damage," she replied. "It's very serious."

I left the church immediately and rode with a friend to UT Medical Center. Chris' parents were there. His mother hugged me and thanked me for coming. "He's in surgery right now. They are trying to relieve pressure on his brain," she said in a shaky voice.

Other kids from the youth department arrived and stayed all day. Minutes seemed like hours and everyone was exhausted physically and mentally by the time news arrived that Chris was out of surgery. The doctor told everyone it was far too early to know anything.

At Mrs. Stevens' insistence, everyone went home before the sun set. She explained that she loved all the kids and that she did not want to risk anyone else having an accident after dark.

I did not sleep well that night, thinking of Chris the entire time. Thinking of all the fun we had playing ball together, going on youth outings and just hanging around brought me momentary solace, only to have my mind return to the current dire situation.

I fell asleep in the middle of the night. When I awoke the next morning, I hurried to dress and return to the hospital. Before I was finished getting ready Mom knocked on the bedroom door.

"Come in," I said hurriedly.

Mom stood in the doorway and informed me Chris had been declared brain dead.

"Brain dead? What does that mean?" I asked in a very worried voice.

"It means his brain has stopped working and soon his body will shut down. John, I'm so sorry, but Chris is dead."

I sat for hours in silence. No tears; just shock. Time seemed to be nonexistent.

The funeral a couple of days later was on the same hillside in the same cemetery where Mark Noble was buried. Minutes before the minister was going to speak, Mrs. Stevens looked upward, tears freely flowing down her face and her head shaking "no" cried out in a voice of indescribable despair, "No, God! How could you allow this? Why?" Not a dry eye remained in the large crowd that had gathered.

The minister began, "A dream not realized. A promise unfulfilled." After that I did not hear another word that was said.

Later that day back at home, I went to my parents and lamented, "First Mark. Now Chris. Who's next?"

I could not stand the anguish, so I went for a long, long run, the only way I knew to relieve some of the pain. I ran every day for weeks to deal with the losses of Mark and Chris. Times were rough, but I was not a quitter. I would fight through the unbearable grief as well as I possibly could, and running was my outlet.

CHAPTER 23

CROSS-COUNTRY AND TRACK

I was a good student and made good grades in high school. In fact, I was smart enough I never had to try hard to make the grades. My favorite thing about high school was running for Bob LeSueur. Coach LeSueur's teams had won the Knoxville Interscholastic League (KIL) for seven consecutive years. Only a phenomenal coach could pull that off. Coach LeSueur noticed every tiny detail about an athlete's technique, even though the coach had very bad eyesight. His strategies in meets were brilliant and I absolutely would knock myself out for Coach LeSueur. For the first time in my life, I felt a true sense of belonging.

I was a pure sprinter, but Coach LeSueur made me run cross-country to get in shape for track season. My goals were to get into shape and to never finish last in a meet. I considered looking bad in cross-country meets as paying the price and I fully intended to pay all the other teams back during track season.

Most cross-country meets were held at Cherokee Boulevard. At one meet I noticed most of the boys team huddled around some bushes near a house. Curious, I walked over and asked what was going on. A voice from below yelled, "What does it look like? Get me something to wipe with." A teammate was sitting on an upside-down grill lid. I plucked some leaves off a tree and handed them to him. The meet went on as usual and I forgot about the incident. Coach LeSueur always met the team on the track, but the next day he was in the woodshop next to his office.

"Sit down, boys," Coach said in a calm voice. "I received a call this morning from a very angry woman who claims one of you relieved yourself in the lid of her gas grill." Everyone stared ahead in silence.

"Do you honestly believe if you knocked on her door and explained you needed to use the bathroom that she would have refused you?" We just looked at each other.

"Go to the track, boys."

Everyone knew what that meant - a quality workout. A quality workout was when coach made everyone run a two-hundred meter dash at one-hundred percent speed. He would wait ten seconds and then blow his whistle and everyone ran another two-hundred at one-hundred percent speed. This would continue until runners fainted, cramped or threw up. Sure enough, Coach LeSueur made the team do a quality workout. When it was finished, everyone prepared to leave for the day, but Coach then said, "Where do you think you're going? We have cross-country practice!" The next day I could barely move. The same was true with everyone else. No further incidents occurred at meets.

When track season rolled around, I excelled. I was in competition shape and with Coach LeSueur's help I became the second-fastest sprinter on the team. During track season I got my payback against the other teams. Depending on the opponents, I ran the one-hundred meter dash, the two-hundred, four-hundred, four-by-one-hundred relay, four-by-two-hundred relay or the four-by-four-hundred relay. I loved the two-hundred meter dash but absolutely hated running the four-hundred. The four-hundred was known as the most difficult race in a meet because one had to sprint the entire time and doing so was both extremely difficult and exhausting.

On a hot, humid spring day, dark clouds rolled in and the wind began to blow during practice. The temperature quickly dropped and thunder could be heard nearby. Coach LeSueur was leaning on the steel rails of the football stadium when I saw a huge bolt of lightning strike less than a mile away. "Coach," I said, "It's lightning!" Coach LeSueur looked down at me and asked, "Have you ever seen lightning strike anything moving?" I thought for a moment and then replied, "No, sir."

"Run!" Coach yelled. I took off running not sure whether to laugh or fear for my life. When a bolt almost hit the field Coach LeSueur reluctantly moved practice indoors. Everyone ran up the two flights of stairs from the gym level of the school to the main level and then back down, down the hall, and back and then repeated as many times as possible. Coach stood in front of an all-glass wall. When small tree branches began striking the glass almost hard enough to break it, coach allowed practice to continue in the gym.

It turned out a small tornado was on the ground, but Coach LeSueur was not going to let that stop practice. He was a hard-nosed coach and everyone absolutely loved him.

Coach LeSueur taught me a very good lesson one day. The team was to run from the school westward down Kingston Pike to Ebenezer Road, then to Peters Road before taking a left onto Westland Drive to Gallaher View Road and back to the school, a run of about seven miles. Every member of the track team took a short cut by running up the hill at Ebenezer Road except for me. I did as coach had instructed. The following morning I was sitting in Coach LeSueur's office and coach could tell I was angry.

"John, do you think I'm stupid?" asked Coach LeSueur.

"Of course not, sir." I replied a bit surprised.

Coach LeSueur c,ntinued, "Do you honestly believe I don't know you were the only one who followed directions yesterday? There was no way those boys could have run that course as fast as they did. Their punishment will come when they get their butts kicked in a meet and your reward will be when you win at the meets. So, quit feeling sorry for yourself."

"Yes, sir." I replied, knowing coach was, as usual, correct.

In the spring of 1978 I was preparing to run in the largest meet of my life, the Baylor Relays in Chattanooga. The meet was scheduled to end by nine o'clock in the evening, but it was still going strong at midnight. I was to run the first leg of the four-by-four-hundred meter relay, the final event of the meet, but I had not eaten in many hours and had a terrible headache. I approached Coach LeSueur and told him about how I was feeling. Coach LeSueur replied, "You know what the best thing for a terrible headache is? A fast four-hundred. Get out there!"

I was not happy, but took my position at the starting line. By the time the officials had lined the relay teams up, my headache had become worse and I had become angry at the world. The starting pistol fired and I took off at full speed, furious I had been made to run. I flew through the first two-hundred meters and was still at full speed at the three-hundred meter mark. About that time I felt numbness in my hands and feet. It quickly spread to my arms and legs, but I was so determined to finish strong that I pushed myself even harder. With about eighty meters to go, everything became blurry to me and the track seemed to move from side to side. I looked at my relay teammate in the distance, who seemed to be sliding back and forth, like a pendulum. I knew I had to stay in my lane and remembered the running techniques Coach LeSueur had taught me and how they felt. For the remainder of the race, I ran by feel, as my vision became increasingly worse.

As I arrived for the baton exchange, I stuck the aluminum baton out in front of me. I felt someone grab it, released my grip, and immediately fell to both knees, crashing onto my forearms and resting my head on the track. As the seconds passed by, I could hear the other runners making their baton exchanges and almost immediately afterward, on the verge of passing out I heard a gruff official's voice command, "Clear the track!" I forced myself up and staggered onto the grassy infield where I collapsed face down in the soft, cool green grass. I felt as if my entire body was spinning.

Then I heard the voices of some members of the girls track team asking if I was all right. I managed to roll over with their assistance but continued to feel the spinning sensation for a few more moments. The girls helped me stand up, but I fell back to my knees where I remained for a minute or so. I finally was able to stand with the girls' help, but I had missed seeing the remainder of the relay.

The race had ended and I had no idea where our relay team had finished. A race official approached me, handed me four gold medals and said, "Great race kid. Your team won." I accepted the medals for the team but was too tired to reply. At that moment, the rest of the relay team and a couple of team managers surrounded me, hugging and patting me on the back, almost knocking my exhausted body down. "Man!" exclaimed one of the managers, "your split was 47.7! We all thought you would tighten up but you didn't. Fantastic run!"

Just as life had been, the race was extremely challenging, but I had persevered. I won a gold medal and was very happy and proud. Instead of anger, I felt an overwhelming sense of gratitude that Coach LeSueur forced me to rise above my circumstances. It was a life lesson I would never forget.

My fondest memories of high school were my days running for the incredible Coach Bob LeSueur.

As high school graduation drew near, I knew life would not be easy, as it never had been, but I knew without a doubt that perseverance, empathy and faith would see me through.